Daryl Van Horne **IS** Santa Claus

Also includes: EARWIG

Author's Note:
I did Twitter for about 37 seconds before I'd determined that it is pretty much a cesspool teeming with idiots. Nonetheless, I tweeted to a guy who had launched a noble, nationally advertised, goodwill effort to get people to each write their own novel. I tweeted: Do you really believe we need to encourage more people to write more books?
As far as I know, he never tweeted back.

The lengthy childish rant that followed only ended when I found myself snarling, "And the last thing we need is another stupid Christmas story!" Naturally, I started work on this one right away.

ESTUARY PUBLICATIONS

© 2022 estuarypublications.com
Grass Valley, CA
ISBN: 9781723863240

EstuaryPublications.com has the permission of *Bob Dylan Music Company* (*Special Rider Music*) to use the Bob Dylan songs mentioned in Daryl Van Horne IS Santa Claus, in this highly speculative manner.

Daryl Van Horne **IS** SANTA CLAUS

adapted from the screenplay by
Darryl Mockridge

DECEMBER 26

It's late afternoon on the day after Christmas, inside a typical New Jersey tavern. Typical, you know, cracked green vinyl floors, heavy captain's chairs in bad repair, huge dark, ornate wooden back bar with a very large mirror, and, above the cash register, a clock with a cowgirl in a short, fringed skirt and matching vest, lifting a cold beer to her lips under a full, bright yellow moon.

The door to the tavern blows open and Santa—dressed in a long, exaggerated fur coat—strolls in just as if he might own the place. (He doesn't.) Santa looks A LOT like Jack Nicholson. He SOUNDS like Jack Nicholson too. He takes off the fur and tosses it onto a coat rack near the door. Underneath he is wearing a very nicely fitted tuxedo. Proudly he poses, arms extended, prepared to welcome admirers into his open, loving embrace.

The place is completely empty. Santa looks around, as if disappointed by the poor turn out, but he resigns himself. In an instant he's jovial again.
"Well, I'd say it's another successful little outing for the old man," Santa declares proudly. He sits down at a table.

Tony, the barkeep and owner, leans almost lifelessly against the back counter. He is a slightly bowed, trim, if bedraggled, man of 37. He looks like he's already gone 14 rounds in the ring with a particularly brutal Life and has taken a serious beating in every round. He has a towel in one hand. He looks at it, smirks and, as if recognizing the metaphor, tosses the towel across the bar onto the floor. It's a futile gesture; Life goes on, dragging Tony along with it. He's completely uninterested in Santa's antics but tends his professional obligations.
"Things went well, did they?" he asks with no indication that an answer might either be required or mean anything at all to him.

Santa's energetic but humble.
"I think so. I think so." He pushes his chair away from the table. He puts his hands behind his head, leans back in the chair. "And how are things with you, Anthony?"

"Fine."
"Well, you say *fine*, but I don't hear it. I don't really *feel it,* Anthony. It lacks the ring of authenticity. Did you have a nice Christmas? Santa bring you everything you wanted?"
"I stopped believing in Santa Claus a few years back."
Santa sighs.

"Well, that's your mistake, Tone. You need to KEEP believin'. You need to BELIEVE in the unbelievable. What else is there?" Santa looks around at the empty dive. "I'll have my champagne now, if you don't mind." Santa puts his exquisite calf's skin boots up on the tabletop.

On his way across the floor, carrying an ice bucket with a champagne bottle and one glass, Tony is mumbling to himself, "If there was a Santa Claus, I'd ask him to burn this fuckin' tavern to the ground, and the whole goddamned miserable neighborhood along with it."
Santa overhears this, smiles and nods sympathetically.
Tony places the bottle and glass on the table and forces a grin.

"Thank you, Tone; and bring another glass…you never know when it might come in handy… right now f'r instance."
To make his point, he looks around at the empty place.
Tony follows his gaze and glances at the door with little hope.

"There's no one here but just you and me, Tone—as they say in the song. Have a little of the bubbly with your oldest, dearest, and most dedicated customer. Now's your chance; tomorrow it's back to beer."
Santa removes one leg from the table and kicks a chair toward Tony.
"Take a load off."
"You're serious?" Tony snorts.
"Would I kid about a thing of such monumental import? Have a seat."
He nudges the chair out a little further toward the barkeep.
The barkeep hesitates. Santa's disappointed that his offer is not taken up immediately.
"Tone! I been comin' in here on the day after Christmas even before your granddad owned this joint. I've spent almost every day in here from December 26 until July 18th for as long as anyone can remember, and you won't sit down and have a little drink with me?"

He removes his leg from the table and eyes the barkeep accusatorily. "Don't you care about me, Tone? Don't you want to hear what I'm thinkin'? That don't seem right. I care about *you*; I care about what *you're* thinkin', and I care about what you're up to, Anthony." Santa leans toward the barkeep. "I also understand what you're up against." He gestures toward the empty bar. "BUT," Santa continues, "do what you gotta do."
Santa pours a glass for himself and elevates it toward the light overhead to admire. He drinks with great luxury.

"I have to say this though, Tone. Have *you* ever *once* looked up and smiled at me? Have you ever taken the time to say, 'Welcome back!'? Have you ever asked me what's goin' on in this noggin' of mine?" Santa sighs again, but this time more deeply. "If I was the sensitive sort, I might reasonably be offended, Anthony. Have a seat, let's talk; I'll tell you a little secret… somethin' nobody else knows about me."
"I…uh…" Tony looks around and finds no excuse not to.
"Come on. Let's get to know each other a little." Santa pleads. "I know what you do for a living; it only seems fair that, after all these years, I should tell you what I do."
"I know what you do," says the barkeep bitterly.

Santa is clearly startled by this statement.
"Really? Well, Tone, I gotta admit, I'm a bit surprised. So, what is it you think I do?"
Tony responds immediately, and with some disdain, "You're a racketeer of some sort."
Santa laughs. "Racketeer? Well, there's a word you don't hear every day. Well, Anthony, I gotta admit, you're pretty close. And I thought I had you fooled." He raises a glass and drinks. "Here's to perception."

Tony goes back behind the bar as Santa raises the glass again, this time more slowly, more elegantly and, chuckling to himself, brings the glass to his greedily smacking lips. "Rackateer… I like the sound of that."
[And, if this were a play, that would be the end of that scene.]

Much later, on that very same night, outside that old tavern, Santa emerges to a very cold, somewhat dirty New Jersey city street. Parked directly in front of the bar is a long black limousine with the driver's side door open. The driver's seat is empty. Santa shivers in his fur coat, and spins in a circle on one heel, looking for his driver. He doesn't seem pleased.
"Gregory?" he shouts, "Gregory!"

He goes around to the front of the limousine and scratches his head. He leans up against the hood for a bit, then sighs and takes a few steps down the street to look around. There, in an alley, up against a brick wall, is the driver. Two thugs have him at knife point. Santa approaches without hesitation. He's somewhat peevish as he addresses the driver.
"Well, Gregory, what are you doing? This is no time for antics, I'm ready to go home."

The first thug looks at Santa and smirks. "You out of your mind, old man? You want to get yourself cut?"
"What's your name?" asks Santa.
"D' fuck business is that of yours?"
"You'd be surprised. But, let's play a little game, shall we?"
"Does it look like we're playing games here?"
"No, it most certainly doesn't, I'll give you that. But, let's work this the other way around. You tell me where you grew up, and *I'll tell you* your name. How would that be?"
"How 'bout this instead…YOU tell me where YOU live and after I slice up your boy here, YOU chauffer US over there and we take everything you own? How would THAT be?"
"Well, that's pretty clever, for a punk."
The thug abandons his grip on the driver, points the knife toward Santa. "Who you callin' punk? I'll slice your white ass."

At this point the other thug quickly intervenes. He has a somewhat slow-witted Southern accent.
"Tyrico. Mayhaps the man didn't mean anything by it. All we want is the car, Ty. Don't let's lose sight of that."
"Tyrico?" says Santa. "Thank you, young man," he says to the other thug. "Now, Tyrico, where were you raised… what city?"

Waving the knife at Santa, Tyrico says, "What the fuck? Are you crazy, old man?"

The other intervenes again, "You was raised in Duluth, ain' so, Ty?"

"Oh really? I know Duluth pretty well," says Santa. "Where abouts?"

Tyrico, leaning casually against Gregory's throat now, says, "In the bad part of a bad town, old man. You satisfied? Now may I *PLEASE* start carving up this turkey?"

"Let me guess," says Santa. "One hundred and thirty-fourth Street?"

Tyrico corrects him, "Langdon Ave, fucker."

"There's no need to quibble, Tyrico. 237 Langdon, apartment D; that's pretty close to 134th. Old brick place… third floor walk-up… in the back… lived with your grandmother, Pearl. How'm I doin'?"

Tyrico switches his hands so that he's leaning on Gregory's chest. "How the fuck...?"

"Let me show you something, Mr. Bad Ass 134th Street," says Santa, and he opens his coat to reveal the butt of an impressively large, silver-plated handgun.

"That a G-40?"

"Yes, Tyrico, that's a G-40. But what I want to show you is this…"

He pulls a paper from out of his coat, unfolds it and holds it up before Tyrico's eyes.

"What IS that?"

"That's the algebra test you failed, preventing you from graduating high school. Do you remember the night before you took that test? Do you recall pleading, 'All I want for Christmas is to pass this dumb-ass test so I can get out of this dumb-ass school?' You could have had that, Tyrico, but you forgot to say the magic words."

"Magic words?" Tyrico asks, clearly confused, "What are you talkin' about?"

"*Dear Santa*. That's the standard form. You should have said, *Dear Santa*, all I want for Christmas is to pass this dumb-ass test."

"Let me see that." Tyrico snatches the paper from Santa's hand.

Still leaning against the driver's chest; still wielding his knife, Tyrico looks at the paper and begins losing his grip on things. After staring at the test for a long time, he looks up, focuses—warily—on Santa.

"I was s'posed to say, '*Dear Santa*, all I want for Christmas is to pass this dumb-ass test?"
"You'd be amazed at what a difference the proper format makes in this world."

Trapped somewhere between furious and pleading, Tyrico whines, "Man, how do you know all this stuff?"
"Well, Tyrico, I know a lot of things. Let me show you something else, which I just happen to have with me. This is where the true miracle occurs, Tyrico." He withdraws a letter from within his coat. "THIS is a letter of acceptance at the Mechanics Institute—that's what you were really after, isn't it? Well, here it is, the letter you *would have* received if you had only passed that algebra test."
"Letter of acceptance… that I *didn't* get? The hell are you talkin' 'bout? I don't believe any of this."

"Well, Tyrico, <u>that</u> just may be your problem. You gotta believe for it to work. Have another look. See, that's your name right there." Santa hands him the letter. "You might want to keep that."
Tyrico holds the knife in one hand, the test and the letter, in the other. He doesn't know what's real anymore, and he doesn't know what to do.

"Congratulations, Tyrico," says Santa, "you've been accepted at the Mechanics Institute. All you gotta do is show up."
Tyrico, though staggered, quickly recovers. "Shit, man, you couldn't a just helped me back then?"
"Your gratitude is touching, Tyrico. Now release Gregory and tell him you're sorry."
"Sorry, man, all we wanted was your wheels."

Santa and Gregory begin to walk away.
"Classes begin in February, Tyrico. Contact those people and let them know you're coming. They'll want to see that letter. Come, Gregory, it's time to go home."
"This ain't real; this IS NOT real," Tyrico says to himself.
The other thug, Clarence, steps forward shyly. "Uh… Santa. I mean, Santa, Sir…?"
"And what's your name, little boy?"

"Clarence, Santa. I'm Clarence… an' I was brung up in Tuscaloosa, Alabama and I really like the fire engine you brung me, Santa… you know, when I was little."

"Well, there you go, Tyrico. Clarence here is an example of the way things ought to be handled. Thank you, Clarence, I'm glad you liked it. And what about that football helmet you received the following year?"

"Oh, I liked that too, but it didn't get so much use. My moms was convinced, helmet or no helmet, I was gonna split my head open like a melon if'n I played football. But I still liked it, Santa. I liked the logo; I liked the color."

"And when did you stop believing in Santa Claus, Clarence?"

"'Bout eleven, I s'pose. But, I never really stopped. I mean, I HOPED in you, Santa. You know, I hoped in you."

"Thank you, Clarence. Tyrico—how about you?"

Tyrico is too busy looking with astonishment at the test paper, and the letter of acceptance, to answer any questions.

"Well, it was nice meeting you two gentlemen," says Santa. "Let's go Gregory. Classes start in February, Tyrico, don't forget. I'd give them a call to set things up, if I were you."

Tyrico, completely bewildered, looks up from the papers and watches Santa and Gregory heading through heavily falling snow toward the limo. Clarence stands by, waving with both hands.

December 27, Early Afternoon

Santa is in the back of the long black limousine, and they are passing through a nice neighborhood, an up-scale neighborhood. Outside the limo—the lawns, the trees, the nice houses with their Christmas decorations—sit in perfect, self-assured silence. The only activity is a little girl on her little pink bicycle wobbling toward the limo. The only sound is her humming a childish song to herself.

Santa rolls down the window to take in the cold fresh air and fixes upon a huge cut-out Santa waving from a badly painted plywood sleigh. There are two or three miserable plastic reindeer, which are far too small for the scene.

Santa leans forward and says to the driver, "Slow up, Gregory. Wait, wait. Stop right here. Now, tell me Gregory do I really look like that? I mean, do I look anything at all like that?"
"No, sir. Most people seem to think you look like Jack Nicholson."

Santa reaches up and drops a make-up mirror down from the ceiling of the limo. He inspects his visage carefully, especially the neck. He makes a few exaggerated faces.
"Well, I don't see the resemblance."
"They say you sound like him too."
"Well, Gregory, there's not much I can do about that, now is there?"
"No sir."
"Well, where do they get these ideas? I'm not some roly-poly bearded buffoon. I don't dress up in red flannel and ermine, like some kind of a lame-brained fashion moron…"

Santa observes the little girl on the bicycle wobbly rolling by.
"Say, that's a pretty spiffy bicycle you got there, little girl. Looks like Santa's been pretty good to you."
"Mommy gave it to me," the child responds snappishly.
Santa takes this statement like a punch to the face. Though the car is unmoving, Santa yells, "Stop. Gregory, stop. Stop! Stop this car!"
He then addresses the child in a soft, kindly voice, "What did you say?"
"Mommy gave it to me. For Christmas, Dummy."

"Mommy gave it to you? Mommy gave you that bike?"
"Yes…"
Santa recovers, "Pretty nifty. You must have a pretty neat mommy to give you such a neat bike. I'd like to speak to your mommy; which of these fine houses do you live in?"
"Number 36. But I'm not supposed to tell."

Santa's talking to himself now. "I never recognize these places at street level." To the driver he says, "Gregory pull up in front of 36, I'm going to have a little talk with Mommy."

In front of 36—a huge white colonial with green shutters—Santa pops out of the car before Gregory can get around to open the door. Walking past a *large* plastic Santa, he goes up the brick steps and rings the bell. A woman, nicely dressed and coifed, answers the door.
"Are you Mommy?"
"Pardon me?" She looks beyond Santa and sees Gregory leaning with is arms crossed next to the open back door of the car. She quickly starts to shut the front door, but Santa puts his very nicely shod foot in there to stop it.
"That little girl tells me that you're Mommy. Are you Mommy?"
"I'm sorry but…" She's now concerned about her daughter and cranes to get a glimpse of her. "AMY! Stay on the sidewalk, Honey."

Santa takes this opportunity to push his way past her and goes on into the hallway. The inside of the house is every bit as elegant, as predictable, as the outside. Santa looks around with a mix of appreciation and disgust. "Nice place you got here, Mommy."
"I'm sorry, but you can't…"
Santa gives her a knowing look.
"What can I do for you?" she asks placing her hands upon her hips.
"Well, I'll tell you what you can do for me, *Mommy*. You can direct me to the other gifts *you* gave little Amy for Christmas."

Santa starts nosing his way down the hall with Mommy following quickly upon his heels. "Please. You can't come into our home and… I mean you shouldn't…"
Santa turns on her.

"You don't want me in your home?"

"Well, I…"

"Is that it? Are you quite sure? I'm no longer welcome in your home?"

"Well… uh…"

"Did you tell that little girl that the bicycle she's now riding out there—inappropriately dressed for this weather by the way—was a gift from Mommy?!"

"I didn't think it would do any harm."

"You didn't think it would do any harm to fill your child's head with nonsense? Or you didn't feel it would do any harm to feed her conflicting and confusing information? Where are all the other gifts Mommy gave little Amy?"

Santa continues to make his way down the hallway, looking into rooms and opening doors.

"What? What are you looking for?"

"I'm looking for the Mommy-tree. Where is the Mommy-tree with all the gifts from Mommy sitting around it all photogenically? Where's the tea set, the teddy bear, the Wubbykin Twins?"

Santa pushes open a door and discovers a room with a large Christmas tree surrounded in gifts. (We'll just follow him inside.)

Santa goes directly to the tree. He turns accusatorily toward Mommy.

"All of these were from you, Mommy?"

"I…"

"Where are the tags, Evelyn?"

"I don't know what you're talking about."

Santa steps on a tiny little porcelain tea set, threatening to crush it.

"Where are the tags?"

"Please stop."

Santa steps on a stuffed animal, crushing it underfoot, making it squeal.

"Where are they?"

Mommy goes to a small leather waste basket under her desk, fishes out gift tags, and brings them to Santa. Santa reads them out loud as he shuffles through them. "To Amy, from Mommy. To Amy, from Mommy. To Amy WITH LOVE, from MOMMY. From Mommy, from MOMMY, from Mommy.

Where are the tags that say *from Santa*?" With his foot firmly on a Wubby, he insists, "Where are the *original* tags?"

Mommy is practically in tears, "I threw them away. I'm sorry… I…" Santa keeps his foot in place, and as the Wubby squeals, she cowers. "Well, Mommy, go dig them out of the garbage, Santa wants to see them."
"I threw them out; they're gone."
Santa shakes his head in dismay.
"Now does that seem right to you? Does it seem right that you should switch the tags that say *from Santa*, with tags that say *from Mommy*?"
"No," she says hanging her head in shame, "No. It was wrong of me, I…"
"Well, it doesn't seem right to me either," says Santa. "And it's pissing me off just a bit. What am I going to do with you? You've been a very very naughty Mommy."
"I know… I'm really sorry…"
"Well, I have to be honest with you, Evelyn, I'm disappointed in you. You were such a good kid too. How are we going to remedy this situation?"
"I don't know."

Santa is seriously wounded. He's also weary from having to go through this. "I don't know either. But, this happens too often and I'm getting sick of it. I do all the work and you people take all the credit. How would that make you feel?"
She has no answer. She can't look Santa in the eye.
"Maybe you should think about how what you do affects others," suggests Santa.

He stomps from the house and, on his way to the car, goes out of his way to tromp across the muddy lawn to assault the large plastic Santa. After dislodging it from its support and throwing it to the ground, he kicks it several times, injuring his foot in the process. He limps to the car, gets in, grimacing. The driver closes his door behind him, then goes around and gets in behind the wheel.

Santa says, somewhat snappishly, "Get me out of here, Gregory."

DECEMBER 27, Evening

The door to the tavern blows open and Santa, dressed in the same long fur coat, limps in, hunched over. He takes off the fur and tosses it lethargically in the direction of the coat rack. It misses. It falls to the floor as Santa watches with disgust. Underneath he is still wearing the same, now crumpled, tuxedo. Again, the place is empty. It looks like it's been that way since he was last here.

Santa walks over gingerly to stand among the vacant tables and survey the dismally lit room.
"Well, ANTHONY, another day another dollar, as they say."
Tony responds, uninterested. "That's what they say, huh…?"
"I think so. It doesn't really matter."
Santa takes a seat at a table.

"How are things with you?" Santa asks.
"Oh, you know… it would be a waste of breath."
"I know exactly what you mean. As my friend Frank once said, anyone that isn't cynical about the situation isn't very well informed about the situation," Santa says wearily. "Nothin' leads to disappointment quicker than the senselessness of it all."
"I wouldn't know," says the barkeep. "I stopped believing in happiness a few years back."
Santa sighs heavily. "I guess you're right." He mulls a bit. "Do you ever get tired, Anthony? I mean do you ever just get tired of it all?'
Tony snorts, "Every goddamned minute of every goddamned day."

Tony puts his arms on the bar and leans forward so far that his forehead rests on the surface. This is a man surrendering to the unbearable trap he's built for himself. After a breather, he returns upright, shivers like a wet dog, and heroically brings beer and a glass to Santa's table.
"Thank you, Tone. Why don't you have one with me?"
Tony looks around at the empty place. He stares longingly at the door for a while with dwindling hope.
"Why not?" pleads Santa. "It can only do you good."

While Tony goes to get another beer, Santa draws little circles on the tabletop with his finger. Tony returns and. Santa kicks a chair in his direction. Tony sits and begins drinking without hesitation.

Three hours later there are empty beer bottles all over the table, one or two on the floor. The two men look like two men who have been drinking steadily for three hours. They speak that way too.

"Tone! Look, Tone, I been comin' in here since… when… since before your granddad owned the joint." Santa sighs deeply. "I guess that's already been acknowledged." He lifts a bottle and ponders. "I spend half my life in this joint. And you know, I have to be honest with you, Tone, I don't like the place anymore; I just don't. You find that offensive? I mean I have to suppose you do."
"Not at all. I don't like the place myself." Tony looks around and laughs snidely. "But what am I gonna do? I'm trapped. I'll never get out of this fuckin' place. They'll carry me out in a box."
They both ponder that statement.

Tony breaks the silence. "You know what I wish?"
"Write it down, Tone. Write it down."
"Write it down?"
"That's the way it works best. Nobody'll never remember it, less you write it down."

Tony stumbles to the bar and picks up a paper placemat and a pen, starts to write, violently discards the pen, finds another, tests it. He returns to the table with Santa, sits and, tongue lolling, begins to write. The viciousness with which he inscribes the paper can be heard throughout that empty tavern. When he's done, he holds up what he's written for Santa to see.
"You should put 'Dear Santa' right up there," says Santa pointing. "That'll make it official."

Tony likes this idea a lot. He writes those two words with added fury. "DEAR SANTA!" he says while scrawling them into the paper. "Here you go," he tosses the paper onto the table, in amongst the empty bottles. "Now, it's official."

"Wah-tud ya ask for, Anthony? ... if you don't mind me askin'."
"I asked him to burn this goddamned place to the ground. That's what I asked for."
Santa picks up the letter from the tabletop, reads it, folds it, and puts it in his breast pocket. "So be it."

"Like I said, I don't even like the fuckin' place anymore!" Tony says with finality.
"I don't like it anymore either. Somehow, just don't. BUT… I like *you*, TONE. I like you; I like the way you think and…I can see what you're up against here, wife, two kids. I gotta tell you, Anthony, there's no sorrier plight than a man shackled to his own creation. I know because I'm one too. One as well. Also one. We're like two peas, Tone. Two peas; work our asses off for what? No thanks, no appreciation; neither respect, too. You know what I mean."
"I do."
"Maybe we're both fools." Santa considers that. "If I thought you were the sensitive sort and you might be offended, I'd keep it that 'deniable fact to myself. But, fuck it, you know what I mean?"
"I do."
"Your bones ever ache?"
"My bones, my head, my ass, my neck, my eyes, my teeth, my legs…"
"You ever feel desperate?"
"Every minute of every moment."

"I like the way you put that. You are tenacious though, Tone. You're always here. Dedicated. That should be worth somethin'. They oughta raise a statue to you in this town. Somethin' big, you know, bronze, something… monumental. Without the plastic reindeer, 'course."
"Something the birds can shit on," reflects Tony.
Santa laughs hysterically. "That's it!"
"Somethin' anything that flies by can shit on," says Tony. He ponders. "You'd think I'd be used to it by now." He tugs at his lip.
"You'd think so," agrees Santa. "I don't think I'll ever get used to it."
They ponder that.

"Know what, Tone? We're two of a kind, and nobody just cares. Nobody just… uh, you know… no body just cares. No matter how dedicated we two committedly are, our work is meaningless… devoid of all meaningfulness."

"Has BECOME meaningless," corrects Tony.

"OK, I'll give you that. Has BECOME meaningless. Every year it's the same damned thing…more meaningless than all years previous."

"…and every year it gets worse too," adds Tony.

"THAT's IT! AND, Tone, did you ever consider this—if our work is so meaningless then what does that make us?"

"Bitter."

"No, Tone. Nope. It makes us *deservedly* bitter. Decidedly, deservedly bitter. BUT, and that's a big but, BUT, it also makes US useless. You ever think about that? They don't need us, Tone. They don't need US."

"We've been thrown on the old scrap heap," says Tony.

"When did that happen?" asks Santa. "I have to confess, Tone, I never saw it comin'."

They both ponder that.

"Well, Anthony, here's my proposal, why don't you lock this place up and come with me out to the Coast for a few days? You know, get away from it all. I don't think you'll be missed. It'll be a little relief for the wife as well. She'd probably be glad to be rid of you. What do you say?"

Tony thinks. He lifts a beer bottle to his mouth and finds it empty. Lifts another. It's empty too.

"You couldn't ask for a clearer message from the gods, Tone. You couldn't ask for a clearer message."

That same night

Santa emerges from the tavern to a very cold very dirty New Jersey city street. The long black limousine parked in front of the bar has no driver. Santa shivers in his fur coat. He can hardly believe it.
"No! Not this again. Gregory? Gregory!"

A few steps down the street, Gregory is leaning up against a building and two men have him closed in. It's a direct take on the previous evening. Santa approaches.
"Well, Gregory, I thought you'd put all this foolishness behind you."

The first thug looks at Santa and his smile glows in the streetlight.
"Mr. Claus, Mr. CUH-L A U S-UH…How be you bein', Mr. Cuh-laus?
"I'm tired Tyrico, and drunk, and I want to go home."
"Can we go with you? It's cold out here, man, and me and Clarence got nothing scheduled for the rest of the evening. How 'bout if we hang with you?"
"Did you call those people like I asked you to?"
"Sure did. They're expecting to see me, in February."
"Well, that's good, but, no, Tyrico, I won't take you two home with me tonight. However, tomorrow I'm heading out to the Coast and you're both welcome to come along. How would that be?"
"How bout this…YOU pick US up right here bright an' early. How's that?"
"Bright and early… around one o'clock."

"We gonna drive out? I can drive the son-of-a-bitch out of that car of yours."
"Absolutely not."
"Aw, man, come on. We could be having one of them All American road trips."
"Well, Tyrico, there'll be no need for that. This particular All American road trip will take place in a private jet."
"Man! You own your own airplane?"
"I writ you a letter," says Clarence quietly. Santa turns toward him.

"Thank you, Clarence. I got that letter, and you don't need to thank me for doing my job. But, what about it, you got a few days to go out west with us? It'll be on me; you don't have to worry about expenses."
"You know, I don't know…you know?" Clarence studies the ground.

"What the fuck, Clarence? Man, are you crazy? Free trip to California. Free trip." Tyrico is truly excited by the prospect. "Free trip, man. California!"

Santa addresses Clarence nicely, "Well, think about it. And, once again, Tyrico, I find that your sensitivity is truly very touching."
"This ain't real; this ain't real. We goin. We goin. We soon be GONE to California."

"We'll pick you up right here. Gregory, it's time for me to go home."

Clarence grabs Tyrico by the elbow, whispers, "He really is Santa Claus, Ty."
"I believe he just might be."
"No, Ty, I mean that man REALLY IS Santa Claus."
"I'm startin' to think so too, man."

As the limousine moves *slinkily* through the streets, the headlights reveal a truly dingy old New Jersey town. There is no one else on the road until a small dark, banged-up car appears out of nowhere and draws up behind the limo. After a block or two of beeping and flashing headlights the dark little car pulls up beside the limo at a stop light. The window goes down in the car. The driver takes a snowball from a tray sitting beside him on the seat.
"HO, HO, HO, you rich bastards!" he says as he throws a snowball, which hits the side of the limo with a loud thunk.

Santa lets down his window in order to look for the cause of the noise. The driver of the car takes another snowball from the tray and lugs it, hitting Santa in the face. "Ha-ha! Merry Christmas, you fat fuck!"

The car takes off speeding recklessly down the street as Santa is wiping the snow from his face. Santa is furious but in complete control.
"Gregory, how much horsepower does this thing have?"
"Eight HUNDRED and sixty-two!"
"That enough to catch that young hooligan?"
"It's enough to catch ANYTHING," Gregory says with real assurance.

"Well, let's do it then. And when we catch him, I want you to run him off the road. I am giving you a direct order, Gregory."
Gregory is delighted, "Yes Sir, Santa."

Twenty minutes later, after a good chase, the small car is half driven into a dirty snowbank on the side of a dark road in the middle of the great New Jersey nowhere. The taillights of the crashed car and the flashing lights of the limousine cause a passing car to slow down and give wide berth to the accident. Gregory is extracting the hooligan from behind the wheel. The kid is only semi-conscious, so Gregory leans him up against the side of his car. Santa is standing beside the open back door of his limo with his arms crossed.

"Is he going to be OK, Gregory?"
"He's just shook up a bit."
Santa approaches the kid who startles.

"I was just havin' fun," says the kid unapologetically.
Santa points at a red mark on his own face, "See this? You call that
fun?" Santa goes steadily toward the kid.
"I didn't mean anything by it."
"You didn't mean anything by it?" Santa takes the kid by surprise,
turns him around and slams him face first into the car. Then he pins his
arms behind his back and spins him around to face Gregory. The kid
struggles but Santa has a good grip on him.

Santa whispers in his ear, "What did you mean when you shouted, Ho
Ho Ho, you rich bastard?"
"It was a joke."
"Really? Ho ho ho is a joke? You say, Ho ho ho, and chuck an ice ball
at a gentleman on his way home in his town car, and that man's
supposed to laugh?"
"It was just a joke, dude."
"Do you think Santa Claus would like that joke?"
"Santa Claus?"

Santa addressed Gregory. "You pretty good with your fists, Gregory?"
"Not too bad, Sir."
"Well, do you think you could hit this hooligan in the face hard enough
to satisfy me? One good shot, you know, just as a joke."
"Yes sir, if that's what you'd like."
"I think I'd like it a great deal. I'll hold him and you hit him, right in
the old kisser."

Gregory steps toward the kid who is struggling to free himself from
Santa's grip.
"But, before you hit him, Gregory, I'd like you to say, "Ho ho ho, you
young punk."

Gregory faces the kid. The kid can't believe the situation he's in.
Gregory begins to speak, "Ho ho ho, you young punk." The kid cowers
and turns his head, as Gregory cocks his fist.
"Wait, Gregory, wait. I've changed my mind," says Santa, and the kid
breathes a sigh of relief. He can't believe his good luck. He has hope.

"I want you to say, 'Merry Christmas, you skinny little moron', then hit him."

Gregory smiles, nods, pleased to be of service. 'Merry Christmas, you skinny little moron,' he says, and hits the kid in the face.

"Now, throw him in the trunk!"

Gregory pushes a button on something in his hand, the trunk pops open and, though the kid puts up a valiant struggle, in the trunk he goes. Thunk! Gregory closes the lid.

As he's getting back into the limo Santa stops to ask, "Oh, did you tell that young hooligan where he's going, Gregory?"
"No, sir."
"Well, that's OK, maybe later."

Santa gets into the limousine; Gregory shuts the door behind him, then goes around and gets in behind the wheel. Now, they're off, leaving the crashed car half buried in the dirty snowbank, looking very festive with its red taillights ablaze, glistening fir trees all around and the dark starry New Jersey night sky overhead.

DECEMBER 28

On the following afternoon, they're inside Santa's private jet, before take-off. The plane is nicely appointed in dove gray colored leather and dark exotic wood trim with orange streaks. It has the style of an ocean-going yacht.

Clarence is sitting stiffly upright in a large leather chair looking straight ahead, nervously. There is an empty seat beside him. Behind him, Tyrico has two seats of his own. He's perfectly comfortable, picking his teeth with a toothpick, his long legs stretched out on a table in front of him and looking out the window. Across the aisle from Clarence is Tony. He looks stoic.

Santa stands between them with a hand on the seatbacks on either side of the aisle. He's wearing a Captain's Hat. Olivia—a stately young black woman, dressed in uniform to match the interior of the plane, stands behind him. She has a genuine smile. She likes working for Santa. Tyrico, checking her out from behind, likes what he sees.

Santa addresses Clarence. "You going to be alright?"
Tony leans across the aisle, pats the young man's shoulder. "Flying is nothin'," he assures him. "You'll be fine."
Clarence asks Tony nervously, "You fly a lot?"
"Sure, I flew to a friend's funeral in 1968, and to Memphis in 1992, during the single week they decided to shut down Graceland for repairs. I don't know which was the more memorable experience. Unfortunately, all four flights made it safely, and I ended up right back where I started."

Santa introduces Olivia. "Gentlemen, we have someone on board here whose job it is to make this trip a little more enjoyable. She'll get you anything you might want as long as we're in flight. That's her job. So, don't be afraid to ask. This is Olivia."

Clarence asks nervously, "Is there still time for me to get off dis plane, Santa?"

"I'm afraid it's a little late for that, Clarence, we've already begun to taxi," says Santa quietly.

Tony adds, "Once we're off the ground you'll forget your fears."

Tyrico is grinning like a hyena. "Man oh man, oh man, oh man. You OWN this ship?"

"Your innocence, if well hidden, is a bit startling, Tyrico," says Santa. "I lease this vehicle."

"Lease?" says Tyrico critically. "Only chumps lease."

Santa sighs, "Yeah, well here's a little Music Industry wisdom for you, Tyrico. If you live in it, drive it, fuck it, or fly it… rent it."

Tyrico shakes his head in agreement, "Oh, OK. OK yeah; I see the point. We got word-on-street like that, Santa. Hold it, cut it or move it, don't taste it."

"It's not the same thing, Tyrico, but I gotta go up front now. Buckle up, folks! We'll see you on the other end." Santa makes his way up the aisle to the cabin, goes inside, and closes the door behind himself.

Olivia addresses the gathering. "Is there anything I can get you before we take off?"

Tyrico wants Courvoisier…of course, and says so in those exact words. "Of course," mimics Olivia good-naturedly.

She bends toward Clarence. "What would you like, sir?"

"I jus' want to get off of this plane."

Tyrico laughs. "Next stop, FIVE HOURS, Clarence. Best you learn to relax. Have a drink, man, they're on the house."

Minutes later as the engine hums louder, Clarence looks more frightened. Olivia takes a seat opposite, facing him, and begins to buckle herself in. Tyrico is leaned back in his chair with his eyes closed and a snifter of brandy held aloft. As the engine sounds grow and become deafening, he lowers the brandy, takes in the fragrance and smiles. Clarence's fear grows steadily as the engine noise increases. Olivia smiles at Clarence, but he's blind with fear as, through the window the runway begins to drift off backward and tilts away slowly, almost to vertical.

After they level out a bit, Olivia looks at Clarence with genuine concern. "You going to be OK?"
"I just want to go home."
"Relax, Clarence, man. This is LUXURY. We ain't had our share yet." Tyrico smiles at Olivia. "All *he* wants for Christmas is to get back to Alabama."

Olivia brightens, looks at Clarence, "You from Alabama?"
"Yes. I was brung up there," says Clarence with eyes tightly closed, "Tuskaloosa," he whines quietly.
"That's amazing! I grew up in Tuskaloosa myself," says Olivia, "Where abouts are you from?"
"Creekside," says Clarence between clenched teeth. "Wrongside; right there where the E line goes over the bridge."
"You lived in Creekside? How did you end up here, with Santa?"
"How'd a Tuskaloosa girl end up workin' fo' Santa Claus?" he asks.
"Well, he's pretty clever… He knows how to make things happen."

An hour later and things are calm inside the plane. Everyone seems to be either asleep or absorbed in thought. Suddenly the plane is in extreme turbulence and Santa emerges from the cockpit. He rides the aisle like a sailor, making his way back toward his guests. He stops long enough to shout back over his shoulder, "Try to get above this, Pilot! It's upsetting my guests."

As the plane bucks, Olivia straps herself in tightly and sits bolt upright, clutching the arm rests. She's a professional though and trying to hide her fear. Sitting opposite her, Clarence is completely immersed in thought. He's beatific, angelic. Behind him, Tyrico is sitting straight up, smiling a forced smile. His dark sunglasses don't hide his fear, however. Tony has moved to the back of the plane. He's indifferent. This is a man who surrendered so long ago that Death might be a welcome release. The set of his jaw is a challenge for Fate to take him.

As the plane rocks, and rolls from side to side, Santa makes his way to the back where Tony sits. He braces himself against the ceiling. "Everything OK back here, Anthony? I want my guests to be comfortable."

"Yeah. But, you know, I want to tell you I'm really sorry I scratched your limousine. I didn't even know the sleeves of this coat had buckles… Who puts buckles on a coat sleeve?"
"Well, Tone, that's what happens when a man lets his wife buy his clothes for him."
"Still, I'm sorry."
"These things happen. You OK otherwise?"
"Whatever."

Tony ponders what he just said. Realizing the source, he snorts.
"I guess I got that from my kid. That's Gina's entire vocabulary these days…"
"Gina must be around nine or ten, isn't she?"
"She's ten, and deeply disappointed in life. It's *all* WHATEVER. You want some ice cream? Whatever. You want a smack in the face? Whatever. She's ten years old and bored to death."
"Well, that's unfortunate, Anthony. She should write to Santa; I hope she still believes in Santa."
"Ha. That kid don't believe in nothing. I'm goin' broke tryin' to keep up the illusion for her little sister. I told her, Santa better show up soon, otherwise you're not gonna get half the crap you want for Christmas."
"What does she say to that?"
"Yeah sure, Daddy, whatever…"

Bucking turbulence throws Santa about the room. "I better get back up front. Try these." He tosses a set of headphones to Tony, then he makes his way forward. As soon as the cabin door shuts behind Santa things begin to level out.

It's a long flight. Tony looks at the headphones, shrugs and puts 'em on. And while listening to this, he sleeps:
Early one evening in 1864 a coffee bean merchant named Cecil Tal was returning to his plantation, at the highest peak on Tender. His little donkey carried two heavy bags containing the coins Tal needed to meet the company payroll. The trail they were on was long and winding and dusty and steep; it was also the only way between that bank and that plantation. On one side of that trail there was a steep cliff which fell in a straight drop into the sea far below, and on the other, heavily snarled

growth which was then (as it is today) so thick and entangled that it was damned near impenetrable. The sun had begun to drop below the horizon when Tal stopped to rest himself and his devoted little unassuming donkey.

Suddenly, emerging from the brushy entanglement, there appeared a gang of… you guessed it… banditos. The gang was led by a smarmy ruffian named Ernesto Suarez (you probably didn't guess that). Mr. Suarez stuck a gun in Cecil Tal's face and smiled a clever confident smile. In response, Tal sighed the weary sigh of a man who had, for a very long time, pretty much expected to be robbed at gunpoint on that trail, at one time or another. So, actually, in a weird sorta way, it was a relief to finally get it over with. That seemed to be his thinking as he threw up both hands and dropped, with a thump, to his knees in the dirt.

At that very moment something unusual occurred. The land on either side of the trail collapsed around them and fell, a thousand-foot drop, into the water below. The little donkey bolted, leapt the gap, and pushed his way—squealing and hawing as he went—into the overgrown greenery. This left the banditos, their leader, Ernesto Suarez, and the weary merchant, Cecil Tal (still on his knees), stranded on a peninsula of sorts, jutting out over the crashing sea below.

The questionable stability of the out-cropping, upon which they then stood, was foremost in the thoughts of every single one of those startled, unnerved human beings, toughened criminal though they were. They froze exactly where they were; not one of them moved a single muscle for a very long time. They were afraid to even blink, lest the overhang they stood upon collapse. Long after the sounds of their world crumbling around them, falling and splashing into the water far below had ceased, they remained stock still.

As it was rapidly becoming darker Tal and his bandito friends began to inch their way slowly, backward, away from the cliff's edge, until each could clutch a tree, a limb, a branch, a twig, a blade of grass and, from there, make their way carefully to the safety of firmer terra.

Once again on solid ground, the banditos ran on ahead to their camp, hidden deep in the woods, where, no doubt, they spent the night grumbling bitterly about their rotten luck, thus avoiding any mention of how frightened they'd been.

Cecil Tal and Ernesto Suarez stayed behind, closer to the trail—and closer to the spot where they'd last seen the money—both hoping that animal would, by instinct or by habit, re-emerge. They camped out together in a little clearing, and sat in the dark, under the trees, with a small fire to keep them warm. They sat in silence, alert to any sound that might herald further collapse of the cliff and pretended, as is the way with such men, not to be filled with a lingering jumpiness.

Eventually they began to talk. "So, tell me… uh…" began Tal in a casual manner.
"Ernesto," said the bandit coldly.
"So, tell me, Ernesto, what do you want all that money for?"
Ernesto Suarez looked at the man to determine if he was being sincere; and when he discovered he was, he laughed. "What do we want all that money for, Señor? We want all that money to get women and booze and the finest horses."

Cecil Tal considered that for a bit, while insects chirped in the woods all around them, the stars looked down upon them in amiable silence, and waves of the restless sea shattered upon the rocky shore far below, as it had for centuries.
"You don't need money to have any of those things, Ernesto," Tal said good-naturedly. "You do realize that, don't you?"
"You must be fooling with me, Señor, or you must be trying to fool yourself."
"I'm not trying to fool anyone, my friend," said Tal, and poked a bit at the fire. "In the poorest part of any town anywhere in this world the streets are full of women; many of them—no matter how poor they may be—are pregnant. I'll grant you that some of those women may have gotten that way with the kindly assistance of a wealthy gentleman; but, most of them got that way by messing around with some piss-poor local rascal. No, you don't need money to get women, Ernesto…"
Ernesto pondered that for a while.

Tal continued. "If you really want women, you only need to do two things: you need to listen to them when they talk—or, at very least, you must pretend to listen—but, above all else, you need to make them laugh." Ernesto pondered that for a while too.

The calmness and sincerity with which Tal spoke those words was impressive. Ernesto looked at Cecil Tal in the flickering fire light and nodded. After all, Ernesto Suarez had made MANY women laugh.

"In that same miserable piss-poor part of town," Tal said, "you'll find the taverns full-to-overflowing with drunks of every sort. I'll admit that some of those drunks may be rich, with plenty of money to spend, but most of 'em are poor locals, Ernesto. The poorest man, who cannot afford to feed either his family or himself, can always come up with the money he needs for a drink."
"And tobacco, Señor…" added Suarez amiably.
"And tobacco," agreed Tal.

It was true; Ernesto Suarez had never been so poor that he had gone a night without drink. Ernesto gazed at Tal and, while he thought about these things, he nodded and made quiet little grunting sounds. Then, suddenly, he laughed and said, "What about the horses, Señor? You forgot about all those fine horses."

Tal laughed in turn, and shook his head.
"What are you laughing about, Señor?"
"You don't need money for horses, Ernesto. Money would only complicate the process. You're a bandit for gods-sakes! Apply your craft. If a man with your skills wants horses… he takes 'em."

Ernesto thought about that while rubbing his scruffy chin. Tal was right; Ernesto had never paid for a horse in his life "You are a wise man, Señor," he said.
"No, I am not a wise man. But, sometimes a man who is uninvolved can see things more clearly."
"And you consider yourself *uninvolved* in this, Señor? Have you forgotten that not too long ago I had the barrel of my gun inserted into your mouth?"

"It's true, not too long ago things were definitely different, Ernesto, but, at the moment, neither one of us has the money… and that is why we're both still here."

Ernesto laughed heartily—they seemed to enjoy each other's company, these two. Talking like this—man to man, as equals—was a pleasant way to spend a chilly night of an unstable cliff.

"Here's the other thing, Ernesto," Cecil Tal said with a great sigh, "if we ever see that donkey again—whether he returns on his own or one of us sets out to track him down—if you take that coin, you'll be screwing things up pretty seriously for the 34 good people who work with me."

"Work *with* you, Señor?" Ernesto laughed.

"Yes. Of course, they work *for* me; but, I work for them as well; we're mutually dependent. And I realize that the time they give up in their lives to bring in the coffee is as valuable to them as my time is to me. The point is: they work hard, and they deserve to be paid for their good work, Ernesto."

"Ah, but Señor, the life we lead is not an easy one; my gang expects to be paid for what they do too."

"I know they do. I know they do… But, Ernesto, listen to me, if you will. The people who work with me need that money; they need to be paid on time, in full. They don't live like bandits in the woods; they have wives, they have children. Their families are dependent upon that money."

"I'm sure you get your share though, Señor."

"Yes, I get my share, but we're all invested in the success of the crop, and we all hope to get a good price for it. If you asked any of those good people, I think they would all say they are treated fairly by me as well as by the company. Do you have children, Ernesto?"

"Ha! More than the stars in the sky, Señor."

"So, you must have a wife…"

"I have more wives than children, Señor."

"And you care about them…"

Ernesto thought about that as he rubbed his chin again. "I do, Señor; I care about each and every one of them… and I am proud of them, too."

"That said, we really should get some sleep; I'll need to get up early and go find that donkey, if I can."

The next evening, when Cecil Tal returned to the coffee plantation without the donkey—and without the payroll—the workers comforted him. Some of them assured him that the donkey would find his own way home; others—though they did not blame him—thought the animal would never be seen again. But they were all wrong. When the donkey next made his appearance at that coffee plantation, he was being led by Ernesto Suarez… and every penny of that payroll was on the animal's back.

Naturally, it would give me tremendous pleasure to tell you that Cecil Tal immediately offered that good bandit a job protecting the payroll from that day forth, and greater pleasure still to say that Ernesto Suarez took that offer. But if he did, it has been lost in the telling.

We do know this however, the next time Tal went down that trail into town to collect some funds, he saw Ernesto Suarez riding around proudly on one of the finest horses he had ever seen.
"I took your advice, Señor!" Suarez shouted.
"I can see that," said Tal, "What's a horse like that worth, Ernesto?"
"I have no idea, Señor," Ernesto shouted.
"Well, don't be unreasonable, Mr. Suarez," warned Cecil Tal, "this is a pretty small island."
"This is a pretty fast horse, Señor," said the other. And laughing like the (sometimes thoughtful/sometimes reckless/always smug) scoundrel he was, Ernesto Suarez rode away at a furious gallop.

While Tony is sleeping his way through that story, Olivia's talking quietly to Clarence. "What made you leave Creekside?
Clarence holds up his left hand showing that two middle fingers are missing. "I was asked to leave."
"My goodness, that looks pretty serious. Who did that to you?"
"Fellah named Ray-Willard Tubbs. White man. He didn't like me so much, I guess."
"What happened?"

"Oh, we was carryin' on past midnight, and I guess Ray-Willard Tubbs didn't want to hear us black folk laughin' and havin' a good time, when he was tryin' to sleep or what not. He comes chargin' out the house with a shotgun, and he pushed through the crowd, and he walked right up to me, and he told me to stand up, and I did. He told me to put my hands up, and I did. And then…well, then he put his shotgun on my frettin' hand and…" Clarence shows her his hand again. Olivia is aghast.

"He pulled the trigger? Oh, my god. I guess Ray-Willard Tubbs doesn't know this is the 21ˢᵗ century."
"Well, I guess he don't. I didn't stick around to educate the man. I run off into the woods and, after three days of worry, I took off for anywhere they might never heard of me or Ray-Willard Tubbs. Next thing I knew I was in New York City."
"So, how did you get fixed up with Mr. Courvoisier over there?"
"I was freshly mugged, officially welcomed as Ty calls it, walking around lost an' hungry in New York City. Then, this limo pulls up and he was at the wheel. He axed did I need a ride and I said, I ain' got no money, and he said, you don't need no money to ride this train, Brother. I don't know why he picked me. Plenty of us to choose from."

Tyrico speaks from behind his sunglasses, "Don't forget to tell her how much I paid you that day, for riding like a king in the back of that fresh-caught sturgeon."
Clarence smiles. "It's true. We drove it to Jersey where a man gave him some money and he gave me $400 right off the top. We been workin' the streets together since that."
Olivia is leaning so close to Clarence that she can touch him. She wants to, she doesn't. She wants to, however.
"So, you say you were carryin' on when this man shot you. Why did he choose you?"

"Oh, I was the instigator. I was the one with the guitar. I was the 'tainment, the shouter, the singer. All the womens liked me. All the men were jealous, 'specially the white men."
"I bet they were. But this couldn't have happened in Tuskaloosa, I think I would have heard about it."

"Oh, well, there abouts, out in the countryside. Big Night, big time, Friday night fish fry. Things go on."
"So, you had a following? What's your name?"
"Turtle Barnes."

Olivia is delighted. "Turtle Barnes?! I remember that name. When I was a little girl you were playin' all the fish fries. Turtle Barnes. 'Haps I even saw you play, a time or two."
"Yeah, then I was Little Turtle Barnes."
"Well, Turtle Barnes, You'll have to play sometime fo…Oh, I'm sorry. I mean, I suppose that…you…"
"Oh, I can play. I just can't play like I used to. It's my frettin' hand. Took me three years to get it goin' again. Upside down and backward, but I can play. An' that blast didn't do no harm to my vocals."
"Well, Turtle Barnes, if I can come up with a guitar can you play us a song?"
"Sure can."

Olivia is inspired, delighted. "You wait right there, Mr. Turtle Barnes." She goes to a cabinet and takes out a guitar case, places it on a seat, uncases the thing and hands it to Clarence with raised eyebrows. Clarence takes it, tunes it, sights down the neck, smiles.
"Man, this is a nice machine. This yours?"
"Nuh. Santa always has that sort of thing on board. He seems to know what might be needed for a smooth flight."

Clarence strums the thing a bit, runs a few riffs on it, and begins to sing, slowly, sweetly:
"Dis your bird, Love? It got your mark upon its wings.
Dis your bird, Love? It got your mark upon its wings.
When 'sees you comin'
Oh how dat lit' birdie sings."

Tyrico, with his eyes closed speaks. "That's the song of a sensitive man." He raises his shades to address Olivia, "Only time he ain't shy is when he's behind that guitar. Play that Parkin' Space song, Clarence."

Clarence nods, starts an up-tempo shuffle, sings:

"'Come when I get home, my parkin' place is still warm?
'Come when I get home, my parkin' place is still warm?
I know somethin's not right, the light in the garage is still on."

Olivia is delighted, "Oh, Turtle, you are good."

"'Come when I pull in, you're always messin' with your hair?
'Come when I pull in, you're busy messin' with your hair?
And there's fresh oil on the drive, like maybe some Chevy's been there.

It's my house. It's my garage
It's my parkin' space for my dirty old Dodge
Don't want so much as a trace
Any other car in my parkin' space…uh-huh"
He dives into a tasty little solo riff with some difficulty. The effort is
written in his face. It's a bit choppy, a bit awkward, but tasty.

Clarence has a new fan. "Turtle Barnes, you are really good."
Clarence comes out of the break singing.
"Get off that phone and look me in the eye
Get on off that phone and look your daddy in the eye
'Ready got the blues so don't bother tryin' t' lie."

Olivia and Tyrico join in, somewhat awkwardly, but with genuine
amusement, for the chorus. Clarence cuts the tempo to lead them
through it. "It's my *house*. It's *my* garage
It's my parkin' space
for my *dirty old*, rusty old, Dodge
You know it's a public disgrace
T' see some shiny new Saab in my parkin' space…uh-huh"

A speaker clicks on.
Santa says, "Buckle up folks, we're about to land in San Francisco,
future retirement home of Santa Claus."

As the gang descends the steps, a limousine waits for them. The back door is open in a welcoming manner. Gregory, arms folded, is leaning against the car. Tyrico, first down the steps, runs across the tarmac and dives headfirst into the limo. Inside, he stretches out and places his hands behind his head. Tony and Santa are next down the steps, and in that order. Clarence is making his way down slowly, carefully, behind them. Olivia's keeping an eye on him. She genuinely likes the man and wishes him well; you can see it in her eyes.
"You try to enjoy yourself out here now, Turtle," she shouts.

Santa and Tony are standing at the limo now, waiting for Clarence. Gregory tips his hat to Tony, "Welcome to California, Sir. Would you like me to place your raincoat in the trunk?"

Tony sees the scratch that he made on the car in New Jersey, before they took off. He leans in to look at the scratch. He touches it. He stammers, "This is the… This is the same…" He's so confused he can't even complete the sentence. He hands his raincoat to Gregory, while inspecting the scratch. "This is the same…?"
As Gregory accepts the raincoat, Tony studies him as well, and is staggered by what he sees. He cannot believe it. He turns to Santa. "That's the same driver?!"
"Well, Tone, a good driver is hard to find, and I consider myself lucky to have Gregory."
"But, he's the same… and this car's the same…but how?… I mean how? HOW is that possible?"
"Well, don't you worry about that Anthony, we're here to relax a little and forget about work."

As they get in, Gregory opens the trunk and tosses the raincoat in on top of the pleading young hooligan, before closing it with a solid thunk. As he's getting into the back, Santa stops to ask, "Did you tell that young hooligan Merry Christmas, Gregory?"
"No, sir."
"Well, that's OK, maybe later."

DECEMBER 29

Outside on the large balcony of a luxury hotel in San Francisco, Tyrico sits leaning back in a large ornate iron chair with his cowboy boots up on the rail. He has a perma-smile plastered to his face. Even through his sunglasses anyone could tell that the man is completely absorbed by unshakeable contentment. Inside he's saying. "I was born to live this life. I was born to live this life."

He reaches for a bottle of beer on the cast iron table beside him and finds it empty. He waggles it in the air and the young hooligan appears at the huge open French door behind him.
"You want another one?"
"Please, if you would be so kind."

Moments later Tyrico is in the same position, still quite pleased with things. He's calmly folding paper airplanes from a stack of hotel stationary, which is pinned down under a snow globe with a cable car inside. There's a fresh beer beside the stack of paper. The young hooligan is leaning on the rail which overlooks the Bay, Alcatraz, Richmond, the Berkeley hills, the Bay Bridge, and the city below.
"Another," says the young man and stretches an open hand toward Tyrico, who hands him a paper airplane. He tosses it over the side and watches it as it swoops and dives and is carried in ascending spirals for a bit before diving straight down as if shot from the sky.
"Another."

Santa is now standing in the open French doors.
"What are you two up to?"
"Nothin'," says the kid and casts another paper airplane into the wind.
"For cryin' out loud," says Santa critically, "what's wrong with you?"
"I didn't mean nothin' by it," says the kid defensively. "We were just having fun."
"Do you think the people down there on the street, who are hit with one of these things, think it's fun?"
Tyrico sits up, lifts his shades, and comes to the defense of the kid.
"Those planes don't mean nothin' to anyone down there. You get hit with a paper airplane, so what?"

"Well, Tyrico," says Santa, stepping out onto the balcony, "that's precisely my point. Those airplanes mean nothing to anyone down there. If you're trying to engage those people, why not make it a positive experience?" Santa reaches into a side pocket of his jacket and pulls out a wad of bills. "Stick one of these in each of those planes and you'll be sending a real message."

He hands the wad of bills to Tyrico, who looks at the bills with some amazement. "You want me to fold a hundred dollar bill in a paper airplane?"
"You're right," says Santa, "You better put a couple in there."
"It'll probably take us a while before we get the placement just right, so they'll sail good," says Tyrico.
"Well, take your time, figure it out, we got nothin' important scheduled for today."

The young hooligan goes over to Tyrico and looks at the wad of money.
"How are you doing today, my young man?" asks Santa.
"Uh… Can I have some of this? I mean, I could use it as much as whoever's down there."
"Sure, why not? Take a few for yourself, but don't take so much it interferes with your learning experience. I don't want to have to go through this lesson with you again."
Tyrico hands the kid several bills, takes a few for himself, and quickly pockets them. Then they start folding bills into their paper airplanes.

Inside, Clarence is playing a guitar and Tony is lounging in an oversized coach, flipping through the channels on a large flat TV. He's not even looking at the TV most of the time. Sometimes he has his head hanging down over the edge of the couch, sometimes he's looking up at the ceiling, but he keeps on clicking steadily through the channels. Santa pushes his legs away to make room, sits down next to him. "You really should think about the comfort of others sometimes, Anthony."

There is a knock upon the door. Santa gets up slowly, with a martyr-like sigh. "It could be no other way. A man can't even sit down and psychoanalyze his friends without interruption."
Santa opens the door, and a bellman hands him a newspaper.
"Here's the paper you ordered, sir."
"Well, thank you son, I appreciate it."
Santa hands the young man a generous tip. He unfolds the small newspaper and starts to read it while walking back to the couch. He sits down near Tony.

Tony continues staring at the TV. Clarence continues working on his guitar.
"Say, here's something interesting. Look at this, Anthony." He hands Tony the newspaper, points out something within. "That part right there, read that."
Anthony reads it. "Who's Ray-Willard Tubbs?"
Clarence stops playing for a beat, then continues playing softly.

Santa mocks surprise. "Did somethin' happen to Ray-Willard?"
"Yeah, it says here that he shot himself in the foot and lost three toes."
"Three toes," says Santa, "Well, so what? Three toes are nothing."
"No, but it says the guy was an amateur competitive dancer of some sort—tango it says—and he was expected to go to some national tango competition."
"Let me see that paper. I didn't read that part." Santa looks at the article. "Well, that's his picture alright. But, if that's the Ray-Willard I knew, he certainly kept that part of his life well hid." Santa reads the article. "Yep, that's him alright. Says here he'll probably never tango again."
"Tough break for that guy…" says Tony, dryly.
"Ah well," says Santa, "there's just no justice in this world."

Santa sits smugly smacking his lips. "You want to look at this newspaper, Clarence?"
"No, sir…uh no, Santa, sir."
"Comes from down where you come from."
"That's OK, sir…uh, Santa, sir. Thank you."

"Well, there's no need to thank me, Clarence. Sometimes these things just happen." Santa gets up. "I think I'll have a drink. Either of you fellows want something to drink? Suddenly, I feel like celebrating."

DECEMBER 30

It's late afternoon and Tony is laying on his back in the middle of the floor looking up at the chandelier. He's mindlessly pulling on his lip. Santa is sitting in a large wing-back chair, with reading glasses, reading a large book. He closes the book, raises his glasses, in order to look at his friend on the floor.

"This has got to end, Anthony. There's a whole world out there; we can't just sit around in here all week. The kids have all gone; they've found something to do. I'll give you one more day in that funk of yours, but tomorrow night we're going out. And I know just the place."

"What's the point?" sighs Tony.

"Well, Tone, I can't tell you that. But I can tell you this: I understand."

"Do you?"

"Yes, Anthony, I do. I understand that you're feeling trapped."

"Not *feelin' trapped*… AM TRAPPED."

"OK… ARE trapped; just staying afloat is a constant struggle. But now your kids are beginning to see things in that murky light."

"Yeah, that's the part that worries me the most."

"And that, Anthony, is what makes you a good man."

"Throw in $4 and maybe it'll get me a cup of coffee."

"Well, who can argue with that...? I certainly can't."

Santa goes back to reading his book. Tony goes back to tugging on his lip. After a bit, Santa closes the book again.

"I'm kind of in the same situation, Anthony—not exactly—but… like you, I work hard; and, like you, I've grown weary of my work. It doesn't really fulfill me anymore. On top of that, I'm not feeling needed; I'm not feeling appreciated. I don't get the thanks I think I deserve. At times, I'd like to just walk away from it; but, like you, Anthony, I can't. People are dependent on me."

Tony pushes himself up onto one elbow and looks at Santa with compassion.

Santa concludes, "Just one time I'd like to experience gratitude through something more than stale, store-bought cookies."

"I know what you mean," says Tony, and collapsed down onto his back again.

DECEMBER 31

Outside The Holy Bagel, in North Beach.
It's almost 10 PM. Even from outside you can see that this place is
PACKED. There is a small crowd waiting in line, hoping to get in.
Santa and Tony come down the street and stop in front of the bar.
There's a huge sign outside declaring: *You think you can do a pretty
good Jack Nicholson?* WELCOME TO THE FIFTH ANNUAL
INTERNATIONAL "JACK" OFF! $10,000 FIRST PRIZE!

Santa stops, reads the sign. "Hey, you know, Anthony, some people
think I look like this guy Nicholson."
From the way they all look at Santa it's pretty clear people in line think
he is Nicholson.
"If you do, I never noticed it."
"They say I even talk like the man."
"Yeah, they say I talk like some Bronx moron, an' I'm from Jersey!"

There is a young man standing upon a crate with a sign around his neck
which says, "I SHOULD HAVE WON". He's doing a fairly
remarkable imitation of Jack Nicholson reciting from a phone book.
"Chany, Aaron, 137 Melbourne 415 36281…
Chany, Adam, 415…"
Santa says, "Say, he's pretty good."

The bouncer, stationed outside the bar, stops a young man trying to
sneak in. "Hey. Hey-hey hey… Where you goin'?
"I just came out of there, dude. You remember me…"
"You got a hand stamp?"
The kid shrugs.
"Get outta here." The bouncer makes a loud announcement to the
people in line, "If you DON'T got a ticket, you're wasting your time. If
you DON'T got a hand stamp, you're not getting' in."

Several people break from the line and walk away disgusted. A couple
walks up, flash their tickets, and he starts unhooking the velvet rope to
let them in. As he's doing that, he sees Santa and Tony, and quickly
bars the couple's way in order to let Santa and Tony go first.

While making large urgent signs to someone inside he continues to hold the couple at bay. They are none too pleased of course. Santa and Tony are greeted by several people inside, all bowing, smiling, deliriously obsequious.

Another bouncer pushes people out of the way for Santa and Tony. "Sir. Go right in."
Santa whispers, "See? What did I tell you? They think I'm him."

Off to one side, away from the bar, is a large separate room crowded with people seated at small round tables. As Santa and Tony are escorted in a waitress appears as if on springs. She is all over herself to welcome them and show them to a table. She beckons and a third bouncer appears at her side and assists her in rousting four startled people from what must be the nicest tables in the joint—front row, center stage. There is a bit of a scene over this, but the bouncer is *persuasive* as he leads one of that table's former occupants away by the elbow. Meanwhile, the stage is empty.

Once they're seated the waitress leans in toward Tony and says, "I hope you enjoy the show; those people Ron just threw out are the sponsors."

Almost immediately Jeremy, the founder of the event—is standing at their table. He's not happy. He's in torment. He has on a headset, and he seems to be speaking to himself as he arrives. "Please, just do IT! JUST do it, please," he's saying. Things aren't going well. He's frantic because a dozen last second things are demanding his attention, and now this. He leans toward Santa.
"What are you doing out here?" His whining plea is part reprimand.

The people around Santa are all craning their necks to get a look at him and to hear what's being said. The females show their interest openly. Some of the males make a point of their complete indifference—a peculiar stance for anyone to take while attending such an event. So what if Jack Nicholson is sitting right in front of me. I only paid $300 dollars to watch others do poor imitations of the man.
Santa looks around at the crowd of adoring Nicholson fans, smiles, nods, waves a little wave.

"WHAT are you doing out here?" Jeremy repeats through clenched teeth.
"Just basking in the glory," Santa says.
Jeremy leans in toward Santa's ear and hisses, "I don't have time right now to explain how much I admire you or to tell you how many years I've idolized you. But YOU ARE DESTROYING ME!"
Santa is genuinely startled, but unapologetic. "Well, I'm sorry to hear that, but I'm not who you think I am."
"Look. Please. First—you being here is a complete surprise to us, considering how your people have treated me. Second—you'd be much better off BACK-stage, not sitting out here. And THIRD…" He stands up and looks around desperately. "What have you done with our sponsors?" He stands up on his tip toes and looks around frantically. "What have you done with our sponsors?!"

Santa tugs on the kid's sleeve.
"OK. OK. Just try to calm down. First—my presence here is a complete surprise to me as well. I hadn't really planned it. Second— I'm not who you think I am. And third—your sponsors are over there having a discussion with a couple large meaty fellows."
Jeremy looks in the direction Santa points. The sponsors are surrounded with bouncers and there is a heated, wildly animated, argument going on in front of the bar.

Jeremy is beside himself. He's speaking to himself in titters, "I don't have time for this. I don't have time for this. I don't have TIME for this!" He returns his attention to Santa. "I love you. I love you. I have loved you since I was a child, but you are turning a life-long dream into a nightmare, Mister Nicholson… sir. I don't even know if the lighting guy can get a spot on you out here." While he's saying all of this, he's turning frequently to monitor the situation with the sponsors.

Santa tugs on his sleeve again and drags him back down to whisper into his ear. "I'm not who you think I am."
Jeremy, not knowing what else to do, goes along with it, "Who are you then?"
"I'm Santa Claus."
"Oh, Jesus. I don't have time for this. I just don't."

He turns, fights his way through the crowd, and runs to the spot where the bouncers now have their hands on one of the male sponsors. They are about to drag him toward an exit when Jeremy arrives. He's just in time to intervene and offer an apology.

Jeremy is soon entangled in the process of alternately talking to the bouncers, the sponsors, into his headset, to the sponsors again, and to a young man who appears suddenly beside him, no doubt with more bad news. This young man could be Jeremy's twin. Jeremy sends his twin off, with brief instruction, in the direction of the stage, and returns to continue consoling the sponsors.

Santa leans back and puts his feet up on a chair near the apron of the stage. Tony is looking through the crowd—beyond the confrontation between sponsors and bouncers and Jeremy—at the barkeep. The guy's clearly miserable. It's in his look, his stance, his movement. He's oblivious to waitresses yelling at him, beautiful young women passing by, glasses being thrown against the mirrored counter behind his head.

A waitress appears beside Tony. "I have some champagne coming. It may be a few clicks until we can get to the bar."
Tony indicates the barkeep with a nod and asks her, "What his story?"
A 2nd waitress passing by says, "He's a prick, that's his story."

Tony's waitress grimaces animatedly at the other's bitterness. "My guess is that *she* doesn't like him very much. He's OK, just never been happy. Typical bartender."
"That's typical huh?"
"Yeah, they're all like that. I guess it comes with the job," says the waitress. "He was happy here for about three months…" She waves dismissing the man. "He feels unwanted. He feels put-upon…whatever. Sometimes he's an…" She leans over and whispers the word to Tony. "That's typical too," she says, and dismisses the barkeep again. "All bartenders are… Oh wait… champagne's ready!"
She starts making her way toward the bar.

On stage Jeremy's twin is adjusting things, mic stands, a podium, cables along the front of the stage, when he's spotlighted.

He looks up as the miraculously calm crowd instantly turns alive and raucous. He touches his ear, responds into his headset, and approaches the microphone awkwardly.

"Uh, I know you're anxious to see the finalists. I'm sorry it took us so long to set up. And uh…well… we also promised the manager we'd wrap it up in time for the New Year's celebration to get underway. So, I guess we should just, uh…" He covers the mic and looks off stage for help. "Should I… me? Jeremy is…? OK." He takes his hand from the mic. "Uh. So, let's get rolling. Third place goes to Winston Jefferson Wong, from right here in our fair city. Mr. Wong…" He exits off stage as Winston Wong, a bespectacled skinny kid in a badly fitting light-colored suit walks on stage, with a huge grin.

Wong speaks in heavy Chinese inflected English. "It was not easy for a Chinese kid like me to enter such a contest. When I told my wife I was going to enter the Jack-Off she said (imitating wife) 'You most certainly are NOT Mr. Winston Wong.' Then, after we saw last year's show, she said (imitating wife again), 'You do better Jack Nicholson than those guys.' So, here I am." He beams around proudly, "My wife wants me to tell you that the $10,000 first prize had no part in our decision to enter. Third place! Not too bad for a kid from Chinatown, heh? Walk 6 blocks and pick up a check for $3000."

Winston Wong closes his eyes and gathers himself before doing a flawless W. C. Fields imitation: "What do you mean you gave me water by mistake… you tryin' t' poison me." Immediately, in his normal voice, he follows up, "Oop, sorry, wrong competition." This goes over well with the anxious audience.

"Now, I'm going to attempt something very difficult to do: Jack Nicholson telling an old story by H. Allen Smith. I know most of you don't know H. Allen Smith—but that only proves, ONCE AGAIN, it doesn't matter who you know, as long as you know Jack."

This goes over not so well.

Now, Mr. Wong takes out a big cigar and does a flawless Jack Nicholson imitation.

"I was visiting my very dear old friend, H. Allen Smith the other day. Smith had a bunch of buddies up for the weekend at his place in

Connecticut. I think E. B. White was there, and H. P. LOVECRAFT. H. L. Mencken. J. D. Salinger. Probably ee cummings. P. G. Wodehouse was an honored guest. Now that I think about it, I was the only guy there who didn't part his name on the left."
He looks around at the audience to see if they are with him. They seem anxious, but willing to give him a chance.

"At any rate, Monday morning comes around and I climb on the commuter train along with the rest of the schlubs. Sitting next to me is a guy who'd apparently been a guest at a similar wing ding. While the train sits in the station, he's hanging out the window, chatting away with his host. He's saying what a great time he'd had; how nice their house is, and how good the food was. And as the train gets under way he shouts, Thanks again, your wife is a fantastic piece of ass."
The crowd is riveted.

Wong, as Nicholson, continues. "Well, I knew I must have heard it wrong, but I couldn't figure out what else the guy might've said. It bothered me all the way into town."
Wong, looking pretty much like Nicholson might look, if he were a skinny young Chinese kid in a badly fitting light-colored suit, peers out into the audience. The crowd is right there with him; they're ready.

"So, when we arrived, that guy stood up and started gathering his things, and I asked him, 'Say, you know, back there when we got on this train, I thought I heard you tell that man that his wife was a fantastic piece of ass?' The man laughed and said, 'Yeah. She's not really, but he's such a nice guy, I didn't want to hurt his feelings.'"

Santa is applauding wildly along with everybody else. Several bouncers take the stage and one of them goes directly to the mic, while the others remove the banner declaring: WELCOME TO THE FIFTH ANNUAL INTERN'L "JACK" OFF FINALS! and replace it with a sign saying HAPPY NEW YEAR. The bouncer at the mic says, "Soon as this is over, we are going to clear the saloon for the New Year's celebration. Unless you have tickets to the New Year's event please leave. He flexes his biceps and makes a hammy threatening gesture. "Those of you who have tickets, get them out, we'd like to see them."

To someone off stage he says, "You want me to introduce the next act?"

Jeremy comes to the mic. "I'm sorry, we're being rushed. So, very quickly now: SECOND PLACE—thank you, Mr. Wong, by the way—in this year's Fourth er, FIFTH Annual International Jack Off Competition SECOND PLACE goes to…" (He listens to his headset) "Rudy… Nonnam, NONNAM? He's also from right here, well, just around the corner actually. He lives in Washington Square Park with his dog, Mitzy, Mr. Rudy Nonnam. Rudy…"

Jeremy exits off stage and RUDY, a bewildered, slightly crazed sort of undeniably homeless guy, in what appear to be a series of increasingly larger overcoats, ambles on with a pit-bull on a string and a pizza box under one arm. He stares out into the audience cupping his eyes.

He looks down and speaks sharply to the dog. "OK, you sit right there and don't move a muscle; this is business."
He looks around as if he might be jumped from behind at any moment, then addresses the audience.
"Every homeless fuck's gotta have a pit bull… I think they passed that law maybe four years ago." He displays the pizza box. "Say, any of you want the last slice? I didn't tamper with it in any way; it's completely untainted." He opens the box, looks in. "Oh, MAN! I can't believe I been carrying an empty box around all this time. GOD damnit! I think it was Mark Twain who said, There is no sadder sight then an empty pizza box."

Jeremy's twin comes up behind Rudy, scaring the heck out of him, and says something into his ear. The twin remains in place until Rudy starts speaking again, then moves back into the shadows.

"They just told me I gotta move on. So, forget talkin' about this nation's sudden fall from decadence into blatant depravity—though it has been startlingly swift—we'll have to address that later. So, one day I saw this big sign sayin' something about a Jack Off competition and I kinda thought it was just another PERFEC' 'xample of San Francisco embarrassing itself in the eyes of the entire Indian nation. An' I am not saying I wasn't disgusted at the idea, I was. Look at these eyes. Am I lyin'? But then I thought, there's no fuckin' way in the goddamned Christ that I'm gonna put up with this. You wanta jack off, do it in the proper place don't do it in my neighborhood bar. So, I come by here to wage my protest, an' O'Keefe, he fuckin' JUMPS right over the counter and drags me up to this kid with a clip board, some big important smug-ass skinny little fucker with plenty more important things to do besides speak with me. He's around here, somewhere…"

Rudy looks into the empty pizza box again. "Just in case." He explains. "You never know." He shrugs and discards the box.

"O'Keefe is sayin' t'me, 'RUDY, YOU GOTTA get in on this, man. You gotta get in on this. You're perfec' for it!' An' I didn't even know what IT was. O'Keefe was explaining IT to me when this same kid—the one I saw around here tonight—busier than ever… HE hears me talkin' and he just signs me right up. I think O'Keefe paid the thirty-two fifty or whatever. And well, three months later, I guess now they're tellin' me I won the thing." He looks around. "Is that right? Yeah? No? OK, so NOW they're tellin' me it's second place. So, they wanted me to tell you how I got here. So, that's it. That's how I got here."
Rudy Nonnam bows.

"So, now I'm gonna do my imitation of Jack Nicholson—who many people have gotten the idea somehow that I am his bastard son, which is a rumor I never even started. This is Jack Nicholson doin' a Bob Dylan song. If you were here for round three you may remember it. An' I have no idea why you think it's so fuckin' funny either."
He looks down at the perfectly quiet dog curled up at his feet. "You just sit right the fuck there and don't you move! This is business!" He smiles at the crowd somewhat apologetically. "Dogs!"

Rudy then does a pure Jack Nicholson take on the Bob Dylan song, Country Pie.
"Just like old Saxophone Joe.
When he's got th' hogshead up on his toe.
Oh me, oh my
Love that country pie.

Listen to the fiddler play
When he's playin' to the break o' day
Oh me, oh my
Love that country pie

Raspberry, strawberry, lemon or lime,
What do I care?
Blueberry, apple, cherry, pumpkin or plum
Call me for dinner, Honey, I'll be there

Saddle me up a big fat goose
Tie me on 'er and turn 'er loose
Oh me, oh my
Love that country pie

I don't need much that ain't no lie
Ain' runnin' a race
Get to me my country pie
I won't throw it up in anybody's face

Shake me up that old peach tree
Little Jack Horner got nothin' on me
Oh me , oh my,
Love that country pie'

Rudy bows, and, naturally the crowd goes wild, He bows several times more as he and his dog walk off stage.

Santa leans over to Tony and whispers, "Let's go."
"Don't you want to see what the winner does?"
"I've had enough, let's go. We can go somewhere else if you'd like."
"No, I'll meet you back at the hotel…"
"You're a good man, Anthony."
They start making their way through the crowd.

Outside they part ways.

Meanwhile, at the foot of the stage, Jeremy is more desperate than ever with a dozen things up in the air. He's talking animatedly into his headset and running up the steps to the stage, where he begins pacing in a small circle. The waitress who took care of Santa is at the apron of the stage trying to get his attention. Eventually she grabs his pant leg. Jeremy is barely under control…
"WHAT? What is it?"
"I just thought you might like to know that Jack Nicholson just left."
Jeremy collapses to his knees, "WHAT?"
"Your golden egg just rolled out the front door."

Jeremy flies off the stage, fights his way through the crowd, and out the front door, talking on his headset all the way. His twin finds himself once again, in front of the microphone. There is a bouncer right behind him talking to him animatedly in a threatening manner.
"Well, it's me again. Uh, I know you're, uh…well… I'm told we're running out of time. I guess we should just, uh…We should? You want me to…? OK… uh, OK. And NOW for the WINNER of the FOURTH ANNUAL INTERNATIONAL…FIFTH annual?—FIFTH annual INTER-national Jack Off Competition." He gestures magnanimously toward the wings. "Llewellyn Fitzhugh. Llewellyn!"

Llewellyn, a huge man with a protruding belly, dressed only in a small dirty, once-white, t-shirt and oversized jeans, takes the stage. In his natural voice he announces:
"Colonel Jessep. You can see I dressed for the part. Oh, and my apologies to Aaron Sorkin, a truly great screenwriter."

He smoothes down his hair and takes on a slightly crazed look, while pulling a sock puppet out of his pocket.
The sock puppet speaks in a high squeaky voice.
"I want answers!"
Llewellyn responds as Jack Nicholson:
"You want answers?"
High squeaky voice:
"I want the truth. I want the truth."
"Make up your mind. Which is it, do you want answers, or do you want the truth?

High squeaky voice:
"I want the truth. I want the truth."
"Unfortunately, you can't handle the…
High squeaky voice:
"I want the truth. I want it. I want it."
"Well, OK then. Just relax, for god's sake."

As somebody emerges from the shadows upstage and touches him on
the shoulder, Llewellyn jumps.
It's Santa. "You want the truth?" Santa asks.

Llewellyn's mouth drops open, everyone in all directions is frozen.
Llewellyn drops his sock puppet. "What? Oh my god. What? Oh my
god, what?"
"I'll give you the truth if that's what you want," says Santa casually.
(You can imagine the crowd response.)

Jeremy rushes to the stage and, in the midst of the screaming and
applause hollers, "JACK NICHOLSON, everybody!"
Jeremy hands Santa a mic and Santa speaks, "Actually, son, I'm Santa
Claus."
"It's SANTA CLAUS, EVERYBODY!"
This leads to more mayhem.

When they finally calm down, Santa asks again, "You want the truth?"
The entire crowd responds "YEAH!!"
"You want the truth?!"
"YEAH!!"

Santa walks to the very front of the stage, head down. He looks weary.
He has never looked more sincere in his life.
"OK, I'll tell you the truth."
He sighs.

"The truth is that we live in a world with kids, and those kids want
toys. Who's gonna provide all those kids with the toys they want? You,
Winston Jefferson Wong? No? How 'bout you, Llewellyn? No? No, I
alone have that responsibility. It falls on me. And, because I take my

job seriously, because I handle my job flawlessly, and expeditiously, YOU get to sleep-in a little bit on Christmas morning. You have that luxury. You also have the luxury of not knowing who's been naughty and who's been so nice it sets their own mother's teeth on edge. And though my existence to you is laughable and the source of your entertainment…"
He gestures broadly indicating the very event he finds himself in.

"…the truth is—you *want* me out there. You *need* me out there. Without me, there would be no Christmas presents; no morning mayhem; no tears, no squeals of falsified delight, no disappointment."
He looks out at the crowd to see if they're getting any of this.

"I have neither the time nor the inclination to explain myself to any so-called daddy who doesn't know when his own daughter's birthday is, let alone whether she wants the pink or the blue Wubbykin. You call me jolly, you call me *the fat guy in the red suit*; nobody ever calls me Mr. Claus, and nobody ever thanks me for the work I do. A plate of stale cookies is all the thanks I get. It's a slap in the face."
The poor man sighs deeply.

"The truth is, I'd like a simple sincere thank you once in a while… but maybe that's expecting too much. I may not like you, and I may not like your little brats, but I do what is expected of me. I do my job. If you don't like the way I'm handling it, I suggest you pick up a sack of toys and climb on board your own sleigh. Otherwise, I don't give a damn what you want, and it's none of your business whether I'm jolly or not—I'm here for the little ones!"
Santa strikes a heroic pose, bows and bows and bows.

The lights come up on stage and Jeremy is there with a check and a plaque of some sort. He hands it to Lewellen without ceremony and stands patting Santa on the back and beaming, as the crowd….(well we've been through that once already.)

Jeremy announces proudly, "MISTER Jack Nicholson!" He turns to Santa, "Can I hug you?"
"I would prefer that you didn't."

"MISTER Jack NICHOLSON, everybody!"
Santa bows one more time graciously and heads backstage. Here's
Rudy with his dog. Rudy approaches, hand extended.
"Let me shake your hand. That was incredible, man! You sounded just
like him. MAN, that was incredible. No wonder you guys won."
They shake hands.

Santa rubs his hand off on Rudy's jacket. Rudy's maybe a bit offended.
"Just kiddin' there, Buddy." Santa pats Rudy on the back. Holding him
out at arm's length, he looks carefully at the grimy young man.
"You might be one of Jack's bastard sons after all… now that I get a
close look at you."
Jeremy is suddenly at his side again, pulling him away.
"Don't mean to be rude, Rudy, I got business to attend to. But, I must
admit, you certainly have given me something to think about."

The crowd outside is chanting: JACK JACK JACK! Jeremy tells Santa
something. Santa stops. He's amazed at what he just heard.
"How many?"
Jeremy shouts in Santa's ear.
Santa is clearly impressed. "I had no idea there were so many people
walking around out there doing Jack Nicholson imitations. And I have
to say this, Jeremy, If I'd have known about the 10,000 smackers, I'd
have entered myself." Suddenly Santa looks exhausted.
Maybe it's the light.

He walks slowly, almost painfully toward the backstage curtain,
without looking back. Jeremy is concerned for the old man. He rushes
ahead to help him down the few steps off stage and guides him gently
down the corridor to the backstage exit. A stagehand helps him
gingerly down the steps outside. With great sadness Jeremy and the
stagehand stand at the door watching as their old hero is assisted by the
driver into the back of a waiting limousine.

Inside, with the door closed, Santa is suddenly fully invigorated. He
leans back, throws his arms up over the seatback, as two lovely,
elegantly dressed, young women, dive with great delight into the seat

on either side of him. "Well, I'd say it's another successful little outing for the old man," Santa declares proudly.
"Let's go have us some fun, shall we, Ladies?" Santa gloats for a bit. "But, you gotta take it easy on me girls, I'm probably only good for another 8 or 10 hours. In return I promise to hold back; we don't want anybody getting' hurt."

He taps on the screen. "Gregory, take us someplace hot… and hurry. I don't think these girls can wait, and I don't want them to cool off."

JANUARY 1 Afternoon

The long black limousine pulls slowly into the neighborhood where Tony lives. Tony has his head back, his eyes closed. He's feeling like he hasn't been gone at all.

Santa says, "Before you get out, Anthony, I have a little surprise for you. I know it's a little late, but then your correspondence didn't get to me in a timely manner. Still, I could feel that your wish was heartfelt. I hope you're pleased."
Eyes closed, Tony says, "I have no idea what you're talking about."
"Well, Tone, you'll see soon enough. Still, I bet it's great to get back home." Santa cracks his window a bit to take in a bushel of cold New Jersey air. "Ah! You can smell Bayonne from here."
He closes the window quickly.

The limo pulls up opposite an empty lot between two buildings. The entire lot is covered in jet black soot, making the emptiness all the more ominous. There is a bright yellow skip-loader, half buried in a bank of dirty snow, next to a huge pile of burnt-out timbers and scrap wood. It is a sight of total devastation. Santa pushes a button, and Tony's window slides down to reveal this scene.
"Merry Christmas, old pal. Or maybe I should say Happy New Year."

Tony opens his eyes, looks. He doesn't fully understand what he's looking at. What happened here? It takes him a second. Suddenly, frantically, he tries to get out of the car, but the door won't open. He wails, "Where's my tavern? Oh, good Christ, where's the tavern?"
"Sorry I couldn't give you the whole neighborhood, like you asked, but I have to consider the wishes of others. But, HO-HO-HO anyway, Anthony."

Tony sits staring out the window at the burned-out lot where his business used to be. He's gutted by what he sees.
"There you go," declares Santa proudly.
"What?! Is this your doing?! Mother of God what have you done?"

"Do you recall saying, *If there was a Santa Claus, I'd ask him to burn this fuckin' tavern to the ground, and the whole miserable neighborhood along with it?*"
"Yes, but I didn't mean this…"
"Well, I got it in writing, right here."
"Yeah but…this…THIS is terrible. This is… terrible. Now what am I gonna do? I have a wife; I have two kids."

Santa takes a piece of paper from his inside jacket pocket and begins to unfold it. It's a letter scrawled on a paper placemat. He reads royally, "DEAR Santa, PLEASE burn this tavern to the ground, and while you're at it, toast the whole fuckin' neighborhood. You remember writing that?"
"Yeah, but…"
"You recall saying, *If there was a Santa Claus, I'd ask him to burn thi…*"
"Yes, yes, yes yes yes!"
"You remember saying that?"
"Yes. I was drunk."
"You DO remember saying that though?"
"Yeah, but…" Tony holds his head in misery.
"Yeah, but you meant it, and that's what really counts, Anthony. I can't be indifferent to…"
"I WAS DRUNK!" Now what am I gonna do? This is terrible! What am I gonna do?"

The door lock clicks open, Tony bolts from the car and runs to the empty lot. With both hands placed on his head he leans back with his eyes toward heaven. "NOW what am I gonna do?" he bellows.

Santa comes up beside him, "You haven't unwrapped the gift yet."
"What? What are you talking about?"
"You're only looking at the package."
"Get away from me. You must be insane."

Santa sighs deeply and goes over and speaks to Gregory, who shuts the doors on the limo then gets in behind the wheel and moves the car a few yards further down the street.

Tony's wife and two daughters are revealed, sitting on their stoop across the street from the burned-out lot.

Tony turns, sees them. His wife waves meekly.
The little one says, "It's Santa, Mommie!"
Gina—10 years old and bored with life—is cheerful, squealing with delight as she sees her father. She runs to him, "Happy New Year, Daddy!" and throws herself into his arms. He looks up sadly as his wife, with the little one by the hand, crosses the street to him.

Meanwhile Gina is telling her father, "The hysterical society says it was a complete lost." She laughs giddily. "Completely lost, Daddy!" Tony is focused on his loving wife as she approaches. The little one points at Santa, saying "Look, Mommie, it's Santa Claus."
"Where?"
"It's Santa! Right there."
The little girl runs toward Santa but stops, retreats, runs back to mom.
"Hi Santa," she waves. "Thanks for the Wubby," she says shyly.
"Well, you're welcome. I hope it was the right color."
"It was." She clings to her mother's legs while gazing adoringly at Santa. Tony and his wife kiss. He pulls her into his arms and holds her tightly. When he finally turns her loose, they both have tears in their eyes. He gestures helplessly toward the burned-out lot. She nods.

"Did you know," she says quietly, "that our tavern was a way station during the Revolutionary War?"
"No, I didn't know that. Or maybe I did—what difference does it make now?"
"Well, I'll tell you what difference it makes now. Since it was an historical landmark, totally destroyed, and cannot be restored to its original state… Mr. Williamson says we're going to receive full payment." She picks up the child in her arms. "AND, because it was a lightning strike—I don't know why—but, he says it's double indemnity. That's what difference it makes."
While he ponders this news, the little one is tugging on Tony's sleeve.
"Daddy… Daddy…"
"Yes, Sweetie."
"Mommy's pigment."

"What?"

"Mommy's pigment. She pigm…"

Santa comes up to the gathering, smiles and nods at the wife, pats both the children on the head.

"Well, congratulations, Anthony. It looks like you're gonna be alright after all."

"Thank you, Santa," says the child now in her mother's arms.

"Well, you are most welcome," says Santa, and throwing an arm around Tony's shoulder, leads him away from his family, toward the limo.

"Well, Anthony, now that you've torn the wrapping off and gotten a little peek inside, what do you think?"

"I don't know what to think. I don't know what to say."

"Don't say a thing. If this ever got into the wrong hands I'd find myself out of work."

"I'm starting to believe you're who you say you are."

"I never said I was anybody else."

"Well thank you… uh, Santa." Tony takes Santa's hand and shakes it vigorously.

"I do what I can."

THAT SAME EVENING

The limousine is passing through a familiar neighborhood. Santa rolls down the window and takes in the cold fresh air. There is a little girl on a little pink bicycle peddling waywardly up the sidewalk, followed closely by her mother.
"Slow up, Gregory. I want you to pace Mommy. Pull up right beside them."
"Yes, sir." The car pulls up smoothly beside the mother and child.

"Say, that's a pretty nifty bicycle you got there, little girl."
Mommy cringes. She looks doubtful. She has no idea what her child is going to say to this fearful man.
Santa waits.
Mommy waits.
The child looks to her mommy, smiles and says, "Santy gave it to me!"
"Really? Who told you that?"
"Mommy told me. It's for Christmas, Dummy."

MOMMY smiles sheepishly. Watches her daughter wobble away in silence before she ambles over to the limo. She places one hand on the glass of the open window and bends to look in.

"I'm really sorry, Santa. I just…"
"That's OK, Evelyn. You've always been a good kid. Say though, didn't you have a large Santa Claus on your front lawn last time I dropped in?"
"Yeah, but somebody vandalized it."
"Really?"
"Yeah, they'd kicked it in, damaged it pretty badly. Can you imagine somebody kicking Santa Claus?"
"Actually, I can. I hope you get him up and on his feet again real soon."
"He'll be right back where he belongs next year for sure."
"Well, that'll be nice. So, see you next time, Mommy." Santa winks as the window goes up.

Evelyn is left there with mixed emotions, which turn to love as she sees her child on the bike coming toward her.

Evening is arriving rapidly, and snow begins to fall in flurries.
Gregory turns to Santa and says, "I thought you didn't like the *jolly old fat guy in the red suit.*
"Well, I've changed my mind on that, Gregory. Now that I've experienced celebrity, I'm thinking anonymity suits me just fine. As to the job, what can I say, I gave it my best shot."
He reflects quietly, "Now I feel the need to settle down."

"Where to, Sir?"
"I've been hearing good things about a little town called Eastwick."

The limo starts out slowly down the street, lifts elegantly into the air. In the sky, it turns into the silhouette of a sleigh drawn by a team of reindeer as it disappears among the emerging stars.

In the twilight, people strolling on the street below shake themselves as if awakening and continue along their way. As the child weaves in an out of this parade she shouts, "Look what Santy gave me!"

THE END

A FINAL NOTE:

The only thing left after the tavern burned to the ground was an old daguerreotype. It shows the tavern standing alone, with nothing else around for miles. In front of the building, there's a guy who looks a lot like Tony, standing proudly, defiantly. He has mutton chop sideburns and wears a long leather apron.

On one side of the building, there is a string of mules tied to a rail; on the other side, an elegant carriage with a nicely matched team of horses. Holding the halter is a man who looks a lot like Gregory.

And, standing in the doorway of the tavern, just as if he might own the place (he doesn't), nicely dressed in the highest fashion of the period, with a top hat in one hand and a walking stick, is a man who, if we look *very* closely, looks quite a bit like Santa Claus.

EARWIG

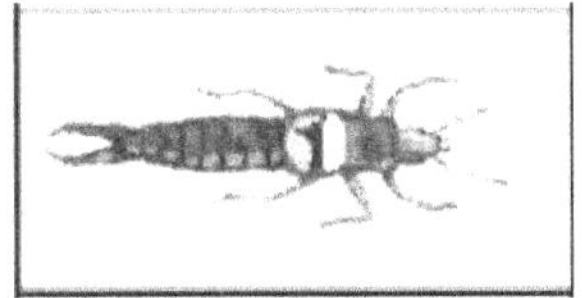

adapted from the screenplay by

Darryl Mockridge

Author's Note:
This piece has nothing whatsoever to do with my refusal to walk
around prattling like a five-year-old, in French.
It has even less to do with my questionable skills as a cellist.
There are deeper wounds, concerning ping-pong.

THURSDAY NIGHT

It's dark, almost black in here. There's the quiet ticking of an old clock. Did I say it's really kinda peaceful? And chilly too. The dim light of an open window reveals two people huddled up closely in a bed, with blankets up to their chins, sound asleep, comfy. There's a cat, of course, curled up in the curve of the woman's folded legs. There's a dog at the foot of the bed. There are the sounds of sleep; occasional quiet little yearnings come from the woman. From the male comes what could be seen by some as snoring, but not the irritating sort, not the raucous house rattling sort, acceptable snoring, not enough to destroy their marriage.

Is it too soon to introduce the fact that this man loves this woman? Henry thinks he's the luckiest man in the world. And well he may be. For him, marriage is the solitary thing in life that has turned out the way they say it could. At any rate, he's one of those rare men who not only loves his wife but remains IN LOVE with her. It's been many years, and he's still in love with her. And there's good reason; as someone noted at their wedding: *Sylvie is well-traveled, well-read, extremely well-educated, young and beautiful and French.*
Then, of course, there's Henry.

Henry's a good and honest man and so he sees the point. He summed it up himself quite nicely on that same wonderful day, while speaking to his best friend: "I don't think anyone was ever able to come up with more than three or four thousand reasons why Sylvie and I should not have married. I could only come up with about 2600 myself."

Though a college instructor and a published book-length author—*along with every other human being on earth,* as Henry himself puts it—at age 58 Henry feels he hasn't accomplished all that he should have. Or at least he hasn't accomplished the things that he'd like.
He secretly harbors three unfulfilled wishes.

Most importantly, he'd like someday to surprise Sylvie by reciting her favorite poem—in its entirety—in flawless, properly nuanced, French. For himself, he'd also like to become a worthy cellist, skilled enough to

play at the very least one of the Bach suites. In his dream that event would take place in front of a crowd of previously doubtful, completely dumfounded, friends. And, for reasons which will explain themselves in time, he'd like very much to beat his father-in-law RESOUNDINGLY at ping pong… just one glorious time.
These things I state in the order in which Henry most desires them.

Henry has failed continually in his attempts to make any of them happen… such is Life. So, Henry's feeling a little sad, not at the moment, of course, but in general. For the moment however, he lies asleep, beside the woman he adores, on his side with his head pressed against a devoted, all-forgiving, ever-accepting pillow. He smacks his lips a couple of times, groans softly, and shifts so that now he's on his back with his mouth open. Don't look in there—Henry's teeth are not all that pretty, and who knows what the man's breath may be like at this hour.

From somewhere there's music. "The Teddy Bears' Picnic" comes up, slowly within the darkened room. We don't have to explain these things… it's enough to know it's there. Perhaps it's in Henry's head. Take a moment here to run through The Teddy Bears' Picnic once or twice in your own head. I'll wait.
(… "If you go down in the woods today, you're sure of a big surprise" …)

The music fades as Henry begins again to snore. It's a little louder this time. Anyone would admit that THIS is snoring. On the pillow next to him, in the dim light, is… what? A small stain? A shadow? A breadcrumb? For the delight of the younger reader, or the still-childish-at-heart, I toss in the idea that it might be something disgusting, you know, something icky.

Enough guesswork. It's a bug, an earwig.

The music comes up a bit to contend with the snoring until the snoring and The *Teddy Bears' Picnic* settle in together, in sync. (Work that out in whatever way you can.) The earwig crawls toward Henry's ear and the tone of The Teddy Bear's Picnic turns ominous.

The song and the snoring build upon each other as the earwig climbs up the lobe, hangs for a brief moment upon that little bit of cartilage there which, like Dumas, I can neither describe nor name, tips suddenly, somewhat awkwardly into the cavern below and begins to enter the ear.
There it goes now. The bug disappears slowly inside.

After the creature is entirely out of sight, the song ends, and the snoring is disrupted as Henry unconsciously rubs his ear with his hand. He then rolls over to his other side. He smiles as he places one arm on his lovely wife's hip. She, still asleep, but always aware of their great love (and by that, I mean their wonderful, fulfilling, exhilarating love), places her lovely white hand on top of his.
If you choose, she pats it.

FRIDAY MORNING

In a sunroom, amid blinding morning light and blooming plants, there is a small round table (I picture it white) set for two. There are two plates, two glasses of juice (I picture them orange), two cups resting upside down in their saucers, waiting. The only thing unusual in any way is a thick French Verb book open in the middle of one of the plates… it waits too, in a silent but slightly more demanding way.

Now that he's on his feet and we can get a look at him, Henry appears to be reasonably tall, reasonably fit, reasonably attractive, almost 60, as he enters the room yawning (not scratching—he's a man of some dignity—but yawning). We like him immediately. He's one of those guys… he just looks likable.

He sees the verb book, smiles, sets it aside as he sits to drink juice. His very dear wife (Sylvie), younger, and better looking, decidedly French, enters carrying fresh-cut flowers. She has that perpetual French effervescence. It's evident even before she speaks. You can see it in her stride, the way she holds her head, the way she holds the flowers. She's full of the simple joy of Life. Henry finds continual delight in Sylvie; the sound of her voice, the way she looks and moves and speaks; her peculiar, somewhat old-fashioned, demure way of dress; what she looks like as she sleeps at peace beside him.
It's not unusual to catch Henry sitting in silence, at a distance, simply admiring his dear wife.

Like the very best examples of her sex, Sylvie is completely unaware of just how truly beautiful she is. Nicer still, she remains unassuming, even timid, as she approaches 50.

"You look lovely this morning, Sylvie."
"No, I don't, but these flowers they certainly look lovely don't they, Henri?"

Henry gets up and goes to her, as if drawn. I don't know why I say *as if drawn*, there's no *as if* about it. He's drawn to her.

"YOU look absolutely beautiful this morning, Sylvie," he says as he places his hands on her waist.
"Thank you, but I don't feel beautiful."
Henry kisses her on the neck.
And I guess that's pretty much enough of that.

For the sake of our average reader, we'll just skip the part where he tells her that she's as fresh and beautiful as the flowers she carries, and how the most wonderful thing in the world is to wake up each morning beside her. We'll skip the part where she says that she is a lucky woman to have such a man as Henry for her husband. Whatever it is that abandons married couples—leaving them trapped in that all-too-typical endless marital snit—has no hope of ever leaving these two.

But, I've been told that the readership these days wants car crashes. We'll get to that in time. Meanwhile, I'll give you a little emotional fender-bender.

Sylvie sees the French verb book set aside on the table. She's disappointed. She speaks.
"Oh, Henri, why do you cast this book aside so disdainfully?"

It's OK to imagine some pouting here from Sylvie, and some sheepishness on Henry's part. Here's the sheepishness, now:
"I didn't cast it aside disdainfully. I merely set it down while I eat, so as not to get any, uh. . ." He looks around for an excuse.
"But you hardly give it a glance anymore." (This would be a good place for another pout.)
"Nonsense, that book is practically worn out from my relentless glancing. I'm surprised there's any print left on the pages. Believe me, everything that's in that book has passed through these eyes many times, and is— well, should be—stored in here somewhere." He taps the old noggin. "It just doesn't come out readily." Sadly, to himself he says, "I don't know what it will take to set it free."

"You must speak French to learn French, Mon Ange," she says encouragingly.

"There's nothing I want less than to have you disappointed in me, Sylvie. However, the idea of a grown man walking around prattling like a five-year-old is repulsive to me, and especially if that grown man is me."

"You don't know how many husbands *wish* they had their own private French tutor." She says this while placing her lovely arms around his neck in a somewhat disappointed but forgiving manner.
"Oh, yes I do," he says, surrendering. "However, I also think there is a window of opportunity when it comes to learning a foreign language, and that window, for me, has been long closed."
"What will it take to open it again?"
"I don't think it can be reopened."

They sit. The phone rings. Sylvie pops up to get it. They live in the past, these two, and the phone is stuck to a wall somewhere across the room, or perhaps (yes, actually) it is in an adjoining room, sitting upon a table. It's a nice little table, round, with a fluted edge. The phone is old and has an antenna attached to the handset.
Henry pleads with her as she departs:
"Please don't get that."
"I must," she says as she leaves.
"Please don't."
"But, it might be Papa."

In the other room we hear her.
"Papa!"
There is no greater surprise, though he calls every day at this time. This is followed by a lengthy chirpy conversation in French. The French-ness of it is undeniable, the specific words however go unheard while poor Henry sits alone and mutters to himself.
"The bastard wants us to go over there and admire his most-newly-acquired collection of junk."

Henry mimics his father-in-law's French accent. "How do you like my house? How do you like my 3.6 acres of nicely tended gardens? How do you like my collection of 14th Century gargoyles, my collection of 15th Century manuscript art, my collection of 16th century Venetian masks, my collection of 17th Century ribald playing cards, my collection of 18th Century hand-carved wooden saints—carved by an idiot, a certified idiot mind you, in Arles? Eh? How do you like these things, MY things? Oh, AND how do you like being constantly, beaten at ping pong by a man who is almost eighty years old?"

I think I should tell you, if you haven't guessed already, that Henry likes none of that. Henry believes—and truly—that life is better and more fulfilling the less 'goddamned crap you possess'.
(That's his phrase.)

By the time she re-enters, Henry is smiling a phony little smile to mask his sulking. That smile turns more real as she arrives. As much as he dislikes her father, that is precisely how much he loves his very dear wife. THIS, my friends, has the makings of either a tragedy or blues tune. I guess it depends on how far we take it.

Sylvie stands behind her husband. She smiles. She speaks.
"That was Papa."
Henry rolls his eyes heavenward.
"They have invited us for Sunday brunch. He would like to show you some very nice crystal animals he has recently acquired."
"How long has he been collecting crystal animals for god's sake?"
"I don't know; he tells me his collection is already substantial!" she says with cheer. "And," she continues while taking a seat across from him and picking up a butter knife, "he says he hopes you've been practicing and that you are prepared to be *crushed* by him at ping-pong."

"How does he suggest I do this practicing? We don't own a ping-pong table, Sylvie… he knows we don't own a ping-pong table. He's the one with the ping-pong table. He's the one playing ping-pong every night."
"We could get a ping-pong table…"
"I don't want a ping-pong table…"
"Then, my friend, you should prepare to be CRUSHED!" she says, but charmingly.

He gathers himself. "He said he's going to crush me?"

"Well not exactly like that. He said, 'I hope he is prepared to accept defeat with dignity this time.'"

"*This time*? What does that mean? I always accept defeat with dignity."

"Oh no you don't…" she sings, and reaches across the table to touch him on the nose, "Not always."

"I've been accepting defeat with dignity my entire adult life."

He whines, "Why didn't you tell him we couldn't come? Why didn't you say we have other plans? That we have somewhere else to go? Why didn't you tell him I was sick or dying or… dead? I'm sorry we can't make it, Henry died in the night."

"That would be untrue, Henri."

"Not as untrue as the faux-courtesy I'll be displaying—begrudgingly—while we're dragged around their place admiring his collections."

He rubs his ear, feels his throat. "Actually, I do feel a cold or something coming on. With any luck, I might be dead by tomorrow."

"My dear, wonderful, Henri, if my father is the worst evil you face in this world you are leading an extremely privileged life."

"I am a simple man, with simple desires and very little free time, Sylvie. I'd like to spend more of that time with you and less of that time admiring your father's latest collection."

Actually, Henry'd really like to spend that time dumbstruck with contentment in a nice warm bed with the woman he loves, the cat who loves her, and the dog who loves anyone who might be holding something edible, with Rostropovich in the background, and no obligations to go anywhere for days. Admittedly this desire is partly driven by the fear that, while he's struggling to become the man his dear wife deserves, she may be seeing only his failures…

-Incapable of picking up French with alacrity,

-Plays the cello constantly without any noticeable improvement,

-Will never compete in ping-pong on a level that will bring honor to the family name.

As said, Henry longs to attain each of these few accomplishments, but any one of them would be nice. Any one of them will do. He would consider any one of them a gift.

Meanwhile, like any man, he has other obligations.

Perhaps on Sunday, at the in-laws, where any French he attempts will be laughed at, ignored completely, or corrected as if he might be an idiot and an embarrassment, he'll surprise everyone and play ping-pong with an unexpected miraculous finesse.

Fat chance, as they say, fat chance.

But, as Sylvie says, "One can but try."

That's the world in which Henry finds himself, strung up, entangled, and dangling helplessly—suspended somewhere between *one can but try* and *fat chance*.

FRIDAY Afternoon

Henry stands outside the college gymnasium, looking through the wire-reinforced glass panel of huge steel double doors. He's watching two students playing startlingly impressive ping pong. The players each stand at least eight feet beyond their end of the table and return the ball with amazing velocity. The ball swoops and curves and dives and spins with each swat. When the final point is taken, the players meet and, while drying their faces with towels, shake hands and begin to walk away in opposite directions.

Henry steps through the doors and says Hi to one of the players.
"Didn't you take my class, Visual Perception's Vital Role in the Evolution of the Static Arts?"
"Yes, Prof. I did. Please don't tell me that now, two semesters later, you discovered I cheated on my final."
"You cheated on your final paper?"
"Yeah, I didn't have the time, so I asked my 10-year-old step-brother to write it for me."
"Really? How did he do?"

The student fakes a good-natured punch at Henry. "Got a B+."
"Really?"
"Nah… he only got a C."
"Well… Anyway. I was watching you play ping pong just now and… you know, I didn't even know we *had* a ping pong team…"
"Table Tennis, Prof."
"I didn't even know we had a table tennis team here."
"Well, then you probably didn't KNOW we were Regional Champions three years running, and second in the State last year."
"No, I didn't know that, but I'm really pleased to hear it. You look pretty good out there."
"Silver medal, State Championships."
"Wow, that's great"

They look at each other for a while. The student has his eyebrows raised in question, but Henry doesn't see it.
He's looking at the floor, thinking.

"So, you know," says Henry, "since *I* taught *you* something—I did, I mean, I DID teach you something, didn't I?"

"Sure you did, Prof. Figure-ground equivocation, warm to cool shifts… all very handy in the world I live in."

"I thought then that maybe *you* could teach *me* something about…table tennis."

"Sure, but, you know, Prof. it cost me money to have you teach me the stuff you know."

"Oh, sure. I'm willing to pay for your expertise."

Henry takes out his wallet and extracts a crisp bill and offers it to the student.

"It cost me A LOT of money. A good education ain't cheap."

Henry extracts another nice bill and hands it to him.

The kid hands him a paddle and asks, "Why the interest in table tennis?"

Henry blows out a long puff of steam. "It's a little hard to explain. There's an old guy who I play ping-pong with once in a while, and he always beats me."

"You mean table tennis..?"

"Table tennis."

"Have a seat and let's talk about this first," says the table tennis champion.

While they sit on a wooden bench in silence, the student is nodding his head while he thinks things through. Henry, always docile, has hope written all over his face as the kid thinks.

"I know what you mean about that old guy, though. Some old guy used to beat me all the time too. So, I sympathize. Man, I could not wear him down, and he was almost 30."

"Almost 30, huh?"

"Yeah, but he could *still* really move. I finally beat him after I mastered the Ling Assault."

"The Ling Assault."

"Yeah. A serve so bewildering that your opponent can not reply. They can not beat you if they can not reply to your serve. Ok, Prof., let's see what you can do."

Several minutes later, Henry and the student are both bent over the table; Henry from exhaustion. The kid is laughing uncontrollably; he's laughing so hard he can't breathe.

Henry watches, defeated, arms hanging limp at his side, while the last ping pong ball rolls off the table and falls to the floor. He looks around at all the ping-pong balls scattered across the gym floor on his side of the table. When the kid finally regains his breath, he tosses his paddle on the table saying, "Look, let me give you your money back. I don't think I can help you, Prof." He's reaching into his back pocket.
"What about that serve… the Ling Assault?" Henry asks anxiously.
"Yeah, that would certainly be the answer, but I don't think the Ling Assault is for you. I have serious doubts that you can learn it."
He steps toward Henry with the two bills extended.
"Keep the money. Let me at least **attempt** to learn that serve. If I can't begin to pick it up in, say, twenty minutes, we'll quit, and you can keep the money. I just want to give it a try."
"That old guy has really got you, huh?"
"I guess you could say that."

Twenty minutes later Henry is covered in sweat, exhausted leaning against the table. He's about to serve. He serves the ball with a strange looking slicing motion of the paddle. The ball bounces, swoops widely outside the edge of the table, curves back in, lands on the kid's side and spins off in an unpredictable direction. The kid swings wildly at it as it flies past his paddle and continues bouncing across the gym floor. The ball comes to rest amidst dozens of ping pong balls at that end of the gym. The student collapses against the table. Holding himself up with both hands, he looks up at Henry through his dripping face.
"I think you got it, Prof." he wheezes. "I think you got it."

A couple of minutes later they are both sprawled on the wooden bench again, wiping their faces with towels. The kid says, "I have no doubt that you will SLAUGHTER that old guy next time you meet. There's no way he can reply to that serve, I don't care how good he is." He leans his head back against the wall. "Just don't break your wrist."
"Got it. Lock my wrist at the angle you showed me…"
Henry leans back exhausted against the wall.

"No, I mean it literally, don't *break* your wrist. Master Ling—who invented that serve—was undefeated going into the trials and, a week before the Olympics, he slipped on some ice, on the sidewalk outside his house in Beijing, and broke his wrist. He was NEVER AGAIN able to make that serve."

"Wow."

"Yeah, wow."

"I don't think there's much chance of me breaking my wrist between now and Sunday."

SATURDAY MORNING

Henry sits on the front steps of his house with a homeless guy at arm's length. They are talking quietly. Henry is saying, "So, I don't know if giving you money every day is really helping you, Walter."
"Yeah, you're right. I really need to do something about that."
"Well, what are you going to do?"
Walter whines, "I don't know, Henry, I'm a wreck. I'm dirty and I'm smelly and some guy keeps beating me up." He ponders. "Hey, have you ever read much Maupassant?"
"No, I guess I should."
"Should!? Man, you **gotta** read Maupassant! Him and Gogol. You ever read much Gogol?"
"No, he's on the list though."
"Man, you gotta read Nikolai. Gogol, and Maupassant and Montaigne; you gotta read him, man." He pauses and thinks. "*By diverse means we arrive at the same ends*. Man, you gotta read Montaigne." Walter's yellowed eyes are bright with enthusiasm for this subject.
"More laughable than the list of things I haven't read is the fact that I don't retain a damned thing. I love Hobbes; can't quote two consecutive words from the man… well, *nasty, brutish, and short* of course, but all the rest is lost."

"If I am a man of some reading, I am a man of NO retentiveness." Walter quotes off hand.
"Hobbes?"
"Montaigne, Henry. He's always right about everything, man. You GOTTA read Montaigne. What are you reading?"
Henry picks up the book that sits beside him on the step. It's Alexandre Dumas' La Reine Margot. He shows the spine to Walter.
"In ENGLISH?" Walter slaps his thigh and goes into a fit of uncontrollable laughter. "In ENGLISH? You're reading Dumas in English? I thought your wife was French."
"She is…"
"I thought you were some kind of professor or something…"
"I am."
"HA! Some professor! Reading Dumas in English…" He's laughing so hard he almost falls down the steps.

Walter recovers his equilibrium, gets up shaking his head and walks away laughing. "I'm sorry, Henry," he says… "but, man, Dumas in ENGLISH!" Walter's laughing like a hyena as he walks away down the sidewalk. From a distance he shouts "You're missing everything..!" Henry picks up the book, looks at the spine, hangs his head, and goes inside. "I'm sure he's right. I probably am missing everything."

Inside, Sylvie positions herself in the kitchen doorway to welcome her returning husband. She has a bag of flour in her hands and she's struggling a bit in the process of opening it.
"I'm really getting the hang of this, Mon Ange," she says as she continues to struggle. "I believe that… this evening we shall have… fresh bread."
"That will be wonderful, Sylvie. I am so lucky to have married such a good cook."
"No, Mon Ange, I am the lucky one, to have married such a good cook." She returns to the kitchen.

Henry's distracted as he throws himself in his chair. He shouts, "Am I missing everything, Sylvie? Walter says I'm missing everything when I read Dumas in English."
She appears. "Well, you may be missing something, but not so much as you would reading Gérard de Nerval, for example." She disappears back into the kitchen while Henry, ponders briefly, shrugs, practices the Ling Assault. "Ha!" He smiles. His smile fades and he shouts, "If I'm missing everything, I want to know it."

Several minutes later, Sylvie appears at the doorway with a book in her hand. "Chapter 14" she says. "Let's see… Oh yes." She begins reading out loud while Henry flips through his book looking for the place.
A ces mots, Marguerite se leva avec une grace toute voluptueuse, et laissant flotter entrouverte sa robe de nuit, dont les manches courtes laissaient á nu son bras d'un modèle si pur, et sa main veritablement royale, elle approcha un flambeau de cire rosée du lit, et, relevant le rideau, elle montra du doigt, en souriant á sa mère, le profil fier, les cheveux noirs et la bouche entrouverte du roi de Navarre, qui semblait, sur la couche en désordre, reposer du plus calme et du plus profond sommeil.

She looks at Henry. "What does your English version say?"
He pretends to read, "Hearing this, Margot got up, went over to the bed, tore the curtains back and there was Navarre, laying around like he owned the joint…"
Sylvie laughs in a lovely, feminine way. "You may be missing something," she says, and turns to go back to baking bread.

Sylvie, in the early afternoon, sun-lit kitchen is measuring dry ingredients according to a big book she has propped open on the table before several bowls. There's mumbling coming from the living room. It's Henry. She stops, listens, goes to the door, leans in the doorway wiping flour on her apron.

It's Henry. "… and have already thus, by that action, resisted the sovereign power *unjustly*, and also by that action, at once, though it be right in the man's own eyes, his tuition being founded upon ancient texts and recognized within the common-weal as they have for ages, in either case *no longer*…"
"What are you doing, Henri?"
"Quoting Hobbes."
"Yes, but WHY are you quoting Hobbes?"
"Because I can. No book; it's pure memory."
"How much Hobbes do you intend to quote from pure memory?"
"Well, I don't know. I haven't thought about it. I'm still fascinated by the discovery that I can quote Hobbes at all."
"I'm amazed that you should wish to."
"Well, there's certainly that…"

She turns and disappears again into the kitchen, with a smile on her face.
"I haven't even read Hobbes in years!" Henry shouts with great pride and tremendous delight. "I didn't think I remembered any Hobbes! Now I seem to remember every word of it." To himself he says, "It makes no sense."

She appears again in the doorway, with a bread bowl resting upon one hip. "When you've finished quoting Hobbes, can you help me get something down from a high shelf?"

SUNDAY, at the in-laws

In the large, bright, marble foyer, a tall old man of excessive dignity—
M. Bouleau, Henry's father-in-law—is on his knees comforting Momo,
the dog-in-law. Momo lies stretched across the width of the hallway.
Bouleau is casually dressed—no tie, no jacket. Henry, nicely dressed in
both tie and jacket (and sweating), stands on the opposite side of the
reclining dog. The animal is a battleline. M. Bouleau stands up, good-
naturedly. He continues to coo down to the dog. "Bébé… Pauvre
Momo."

He addresses Henry coldly, "Momo is here waiting only to greet you,
and yet, you have no greeting for him? Perhaps you do not like my dog,
Henri?"
"I don't like the fact that my wife has to jump over him, in order to
enter your house, every time we come here. She could have broken her
neck in that fall."
Bouleau dismisses this. "Paaah! She was not harmed. But, this dog, he
was disturbed. And why should he be? This is his home."
"Yes, and my wife, *your daughter*, and I are guests here," says Henry.

"Exactly. You are our guests. But let me ask you something. If I were a
guest in your house, would I be free to come in and arrange things to
my liking? No. I would come in, and I would look around, and I would
APPRECIATE your fine things, and I would accept the way in which
you have arranged them, and I would have a nice dinner, perhaps, and
then go away happily. I would thank you for showing me a pleasant
evening. I would not enter your house and insist that you change things
around for my convenience. I would be a guest, a true guest and…
perhaps my wife and I would talk a bit behind your back, certainly, that
is natural… but I would NEVER, as a guest in your home, ask you to
change one single thing about the awful way in which you have chosen
to decorate your little hovel, or to adjust the way in which you live your
lives, or to ask you to remove your cat so that I might sit down in the
place where she is in repose upon your couch."

Of course, there is very little anyone can say to that, and Henry wisely
says nothing.

But, M. Bouleau has more to say. "Is your wife—my daughter as you say—an invalid?"
"NO, she's not, and you know she is not."
"Well, then she can do as all our guests do when this dog is stretched out nicely upon this cool tile floor… she can go around. Simply go around."
"There's not much room in this hallway to go around."

"Well, your wife is quite young still—much younger than yourself for example—and she is capable of taking a little leap perhaps? If my wife or I must pass through this hall and this fine animal is stretched out nicely, in a most luxurious and restful manner, we would not disturb this dog, we would take a little leap. My wife and I are both much older than yourself and your wife—though you have chosen, at this moment to act like a cranky old gentleman… though not so gentle, and not so much of a man—but, either way, we would simply go around or take a little leap over the creature. It is not a problem; it is only a problem if you make it one. But that your wife should choose instead to step on my poor Momo, and in that process come crashing to the floor, is not the dog's fault. Your wife is not blind I suppose?"
"No, she is not. This is absurd."

The dog raises his head languidly to determine the nature of this prolonged disturbance to his rest. M. Bouleau looks down and comforts the animal, "Momo, mon beau." Then he returns to Henry.

"Well, if she is not blind then she could see this dog. And I know her to be an intelligent young lady. She knows this dog and she knows that he lives here. She knows his tendencies. She knows that she may find him here in this hall, in repose. I do not know what the problem could be."
"The problem is that your *goddamned* dog is lying right in the middle of the *goddamned* floor," says Henry, perhaps with too much emphasis.

M. Bouleau studies his son-in-law with the greatest sympathy for a bit, before speaking in the kindest voice.
"Oh, my very dear Henri, why should it come to this? I have not raised my voice with you. I have not used foul language in discussing this

very small matter. There is no reason for that sort of behavior here in my house, where you are an honored guest. Please, come in, and let us discuss this no further. Please… please…" He bows a little.
The dog raises his head again, as if to say, 'Get it over with', and eyes Henry as he steps over him.

Bouleau ushers Henry into the kitchen where Sylvie is sitting at a table. Madame Bouleau—looking much like a woman on a tightrope—is carrying a china laden tray toward the table. It rattles with each step she takes. She smiles with genuine delight when she sees Henry.
"Bonjour, Henri," she sings.
She puts down the tray, goes to him and kisses him on both cheeks.
"How are you today, Henri?" she warbles.
"Bonjour, Madame. I'm fine, merci," says Henry somewhat sullenly. "It was nice of you to invite us."
"Ah, but it seems that we almost never see you," she says sadly.

"Ah, for me NO bonjour, NO broad smile," says M. Bouleau supposedly to himself, as he goes to the head of the table and sits. "For me, this gentleman—who claims to be married to my daughter—does not bother to attempt to speak even a very little French." He turns to Madame Bouleau. He looks at Madame Bouleau. He turns ON her.
"What are you doing?" Bouleau asks explosively.
Madame is confused. "I am serving brunch to our guests," she says meekly.

"No, not like that you are not. Go and change immediately," says M. Boulcau in French. "I don't like those shoes and you know I don't like those shoes," he says in English. As Madame Bouleau leaves like a scolded child, he turns to Henry. "You see," he says somewhat smugly, "*I* do not hesitate to use *your* language…"

Driven by injustice of any sort, Henry turns to face the man and says, "Monsieur, if I learned enough French to proudly proclaim that the elephant is plus grand que le mouse, would that please you?"
M. Bouleau ignores Henry and addresses his daughter. "He is quick to over-react, this husband of yours."

But Henry has not said all that he has to say. "From there, I suppose it would be the merest stretch for me to jump right in when you and your daughter begin discussing 17th century French literature."

M. Bouleau begins to drink coffee from a large bowl as if Henry did not even exist. He places the bowl on the table and stirs the coffee with a croissant. He munches this soppy thing for a bit before saying, "This is wrong of you, Monsieur. You can not blame me for your refusal to learn French." He goes back to his coffee. After setting down the bowl he stares coldly out the window.

Henry, still standing, and at a good distance, responds, "Monsieur, what you call my refusal to learn French is not a matter of pride. It is a kindness."
M. Bouleau says nothing to this. He does not react in any way. Such a comment cannot be allowed to disrupt his pleasure in eating.
"I'm sure you don't want to witness me slaughtering your beloved language before your eyes," Henry continues.

M. Bouleau blows out a short puff of air, a near-divine gesture of French dismissal.

Sylvie pleads, "Henri, sit down, s'il te plait."
Henry shakes her off. "My wife and I share a common language, Monsieur, and that language is *English*. That is a very big part of my stubbornness. That French is a fairly subtle language and I no longer possess a subtle mind is part of it as well. I do not toy casually with other languages out of respect for those languages."
Sylvie pleads quietly with her husband, "Henri, sit down, please.

Henry does not sit. Henry refuses to sit. "I have tried bouncing a little French off you—unfortunately for me *Bonjour* is a shot fired from the starting gun. Once you've heard that shot, you're off; you want to chatter, and you want to chatter amiably, and you want to chatter amiably in French; which is all understandable. Unfortunately, in that race, Monsieur, I am a cripple."
M. Bouleau puts down his bowl of coffee and says, "Well, this is not the pleasant afternoon Madame and I had planned."

He begins to push away from the table.

Sylvie says, with some urgency, "Henri, please sit down."

She looks pleadingly at her husband. She bows slightly toward her father. "Papa, please stay."

"I have no intention of leaving MY OWN table," says Bouleau in bold defiance, and blows out another short puff of air. And Henry, though he loves Sylvie deeply, does not sit. Instead, he continues with his case.

"And, I honestly feel," states Henry, "that there still are some—albeit, admittedly, very few—*good people* left in this world who do not yet speak French." He turns and begins to pace. "I'm not claiming that I am one of them," he says, in fairness.

"HENRI…please. Please sit down."

Madame has returned quietly and, stands waiting to see if her shoes meet her husband's approval. Bouleau looks. Bouleau nods. Bouleau returns to his bowl. Madame begins once again to serve, moving plates and cups around on the table.

Henry is still not done. "English is a legitimate language, Monsieur, and many people, especially here in the United States of America, use it unashamedly."

Madame stands at the table, completely confused by this statement. She looks around at the others to see what she has missed. Sylvie rises apologetically. "I'm sorry, Maman. We must go" she says and kisses her bewildered mother upon both cheeks. "I am sorry, Papa," she says, "We must be going" and bends to kiss her indifferent father on the cheek. While Bouleau reaches for another croissant, she takes Henry forcefully by the arm and drags him from the kitchen.

They go through the hallway (where the dog no longer lies) and directly out the front door. Henry drags his feet, like a child unwilling to abandon a school yard fight. As they go, Henry is almost shouting over his shoulder, "When we're in FRANCE, I get along better in every way—AND FEEL more comfortable too—*NOT pretending to speak a language WHICH I DO NOT SPEAK.* The French are very nice about that."

As they stumble outside together, Henry continues, but louder, "Here, at your place—as your HONORED GUEST—I'm not allowed that simple COURTESY."
Sylvie drags her husband by the elbow to the driveway.

M. Bouleau has followed them to the door where he stands and waves broadly. He is patting the noble dog on the head as he says loudly, cheerily, "Au revoir, mes enfants. Next time we must play some ping-pong. Oh, and perhaps next time I will show you my new collection, it is really worth seeing. Au revoir." It is exactly the kind of farewell anyone who had had a delightful time might have expected.

After Bouleau disappears inside, taking his dedicated dog with him, there is a confrontation in the driveway. Sylvie has her arms crossed as she leans against the car. Livid, she squints at Henry. Henry, always fearful of her squint—for he knows what it means—attempts to turn it into a joke. He smiles with obvious effort.
"Not so good, huh?" he asks sheepishly.
"I have never known you to act like that; what has gotten into you, Henri?" she asks with limited compassion.
"It was a ploy, Sylvie. I just wanted to avoid another lengthy French goodbye." He studies his watch. "We just shortened our departure time by (he calculates in his mind) 47 minutes."
Sylvie is not amused. She says nothing.

He holds her door for her as she gets into the car, but he can tell just from the side of her face that she is not bending, and she will not be charmed. So, he does what any guilty husband would do, he sings. He sings to himself nervously, as he goes around the car to get in.
A loaf of bread
A jug of wine
A rope to hang myself

And I believe, with all my heart
That's all, right now, I'll need
I believe, with all my heart
*That's all I'll **ever** need*

Henry has had a crushing headache all day and the aspirin he's been taking doesn't seem to touch it.

MONDAY

In their living room. It's early morning, as Sylvie enters wearing a kimono and yawning widely… prettily. Henry is already in the large, overstuffed chair, surrounded by various books and newspapers. He's bent over a coffee table, scribbling in a notebook.
Sylvie is rubbing her eyes and stretching.
"How long have you been up?"
"Listen to this:" Henry says, "Two Steps to Happiness. One: joice. Two: Re-joice. What do you think?"
Sylvie makes a face. "Were you up all night?"

Henry is distracted. "No, no. I got up at around five. I did the crossword puzzle… and look at this… (he holds up a piece of paper) Algebra! It's algebra."
"Algebra?" she asks.
"Yes, THIS, Sylvie, is algebra!" He's proud of what he's done. "I never could really get it in high school. This morning I woke up and thought, *Hey, why not give algebra another shot?* And I did. And THIS is what happened. This, dear wife, is algebra."
"I am impressed, and maybe just a little bit confused, Henri" she says. Yawning again, she takes a seat across from him. He's obviously quite pleased, maybe a little excited. Maybe a little too excited. When he speaks he sounds a bit frantic, he chatters.

"This morning, I'm reading the paper and… BAM, suddenly I get it. Suddenly the underlying mystery behind algebra is revealed. So, I did a few problems. It's kid's stuff, for crying out loud."
"This morning's paper has arrived already?"
"Pas que je sache."
"What did you say?"
"Not as far as I know. It's yesterday's paper. I thought I'd do the crosswords . . . give that a try too. That's another thing I never really got the hang of… but, now… that too is kid's stuff."

Sylvie gets up and goes to him. She takes a seat next to him, leans over and places a hand upon his forehead. "Henri, my love," she says, "listen to me. I have some advice for you. One: lax. Two: RE-LAX. OK? Relax, Henri, slow down."

"I am relaxed, Sylvie. I have never been so relaxed. The headache I had for two days is finally gone; I'm doing algebra; I'm writing songs: I'm perfectly relaxed. Listen to this…"

He picks up a guitar which is leaning against his chair, begins to play and sing an intro.

I really shouldn't need to state the obvious
I shouldn't have to point out the simple truth
But despite all that, too bad, and also nonetheless
What's obvious to me, clearly ain't that clear to you…

"An' then here's a little break…" He plays a fairly impressive finger-style solo. Then he starts to sing again.

Without a 'knowin' where you're a 'goin'
Without a' knowin' where you 'a been
Without a 'knowin' where you're a 'goin
You're only wind up, here again

"Here's another little break.." He plays another fancy solo, a true knuckle buster, before singing:

I've loved me my share of girls
I'm sure they all had names and yet,
The one I can't remember
Is the one I can't forget.

"That's all I got right now, but, up here, I'm still a-workin' on 'er." Henry winks broadly, sits awash with self-satisfaction, guitar in lap. "I'm a workin' on 'er."

"I thought you gave up playing the guitar years ago. How did you even find that thing?"

"Cleverly, as you say, I stowed it, years ago, out in the garage, under the kayak, in a tarp. I didn't even have to think about where it was; I went right to it… guided by instinct I suppose, and Fate. Better still is how much I remember from my lessons. Can you believe that?! I wrote *three* songs this morning. And, somewhere in this brain of mine…"

He quickly bends over the notebook and begins to write.
"My goodness, Henri. How much coffee have you had?"
"None. But, that sounds good."

He gets up and starts to head for the kitchen. As he goes, he says animatedly, "You know, I was just thinking about coffee. There's drip and there's espresso, but wouldn't the *best* coffee—I mean the very BEST—be made utilizing centrifugal force? What should we call it?" To himself he says, "Oh, MAN, I hope someone isn't already doing that. Drip, pressed, spun! Bes' coffee yet, SPUN." He begins to write that down, stops and, to her, he says, "Hey, Sylvie, name a state."

"Schizophrenia," she says, and they both laugh.
Henry encourages her, "No, come on, Sylvie, name a State?"
"Name a State?"
"Any State in the United States."
"Idaho."

Henry laughs, "Pah, come on, kid, try to name one I DON'T know the capital of."

MONDAY Afternoon

Sylvie is on the phone speaking in French. Henry is sitting in that same
big chair, surrounded by more books and notebooks and now, maps.
He's leaning forward, watching something on TV. His eyes are locked
on the TV. His feet are active upon the carpet. One arm is extended as
if to keep his balance and the other is poised in space to his side. He
swings at something we don't see rhythmically, repeatedly. His
movements are mimicking those of the ping pong players on TV.
It's the Olympic trials.

Sylvie comes in looking sad. She collapses into the chair next to him.
"I have some very sad news, Mon Ange."

Henry, good husband that he is, once made a solemn vow that he would
stop whatever he was doing whenever Sylvie asked for his attention. It
has been an easy promise to keep because there really is nothing more
important in his life than Sylvie. It was a good decision made early in
their marriage and it has made their bond the stronger; their love for
each other deeper. He takes one final swing and, from his reaction,
drives the ball successfully beyond the reach of his imaginary
opponent. Grinning victoriously, he turns off the TV and turns his
attention to Sylvie.
"What is it?" he asks with some sympathy.
"We are not invited to my parents' on Sunday."
"What do you mean we are not invited on Sunday?"

Sylvie, wrinkles her brow, explains in subdued, kindly tones, "We have
been un-invited. Maman thinks it would be for the best if we did not go
every weekend to their place."

Henry is a bit surprised. He thinks about this briefly. "Well, your
mother is a wise observer, Sylvie. She may have detected a little
tension between your father and me, during our last visit."
"Still, Henri, to be un-invited…"
"Please tell your father I'll be delighted not to attend.

Sylvie looks at him with a look that says, 'Don't be cruel' then she says it, "Don't be cruel, Henri. To be un-invited to my parents' home is very sad for me."
"I know it is, Sylvie," says Henry and reaches over to touch her hand. "But I've just been un-invited to a place I never wanted to go."

Sylvie is in thought.
"If we were to go, Mon Ange, you must promise…"
"Oh, Sylvie, please tell me that being un-invited means we won't be going."
"Henri, listen to me, Mon Ange… IF we were to go you must promise me that you will not… do as you did last time."
"Last time, I had a crushing headache," he says. Then he pleads, "But, Sylvie, it is cruel of you to tell me we are un-invited and then to say, IF we were to go I must. If we were to go I must what… remain mute? Refrain from speaking in English? Disguise my fondness for my wonderful mother-in-law? Gush over your father's recent acquisitions? There are limits to my love, Sylvie. I thought, I hoped, I prayed… I have to say something to you, OK? To get it out now will help me avoid blurting it out while we're at their place.

"My love for you, which is beyond all reason, will allow no less, my very dear husband," she says simply.
"You may have heard this before…" he begins.
"*Though you try…*" *she* begins.
"Though I try," he says, while looking sternly at her, "to be creative and continually come up with something new and clever and entertaining for you, there is a limit. And certain things nag me, and have nagged me, and nag me still, about your father."
"*And so…*" she urges.
"And so, I have to say this… again." He looks to her for agreement. She nods. "*Personally…*"
"Personally, I believe that a person, actually, truly, honestly, literally, needs only so much junk in his life."
"You really should spend more time thinking about other things, Henri."
Henry, undaunted continues with his well-worn speech.

"I believe that life is better, richer, deeper, purer, fuller in almost every way, if you spend a little more time appreciating the junk you already have and less time longing for more junk."
"And this, dear Henri, sounds very much like something, I may have heard before."
He pauses. He sighs.
"*I have always wondered,*" she coaxes, with appropriate gestures.

"I have always wondered why a man, like your father, should continue to shrug on the old armor and throw himself into the daily fray only to gain greater riches in order ONLY to add more junk to his already cluttered life, when he could instead, say, place himself in a very nice, very comfortable, nicely lit and delicately ventilated room and begin quietly reading—without constant interruption—all the books that he's been yearning, for years, to read."
That thought finally complete, he looks to his lovely, forbearing wife for a response.

"I think this is a reasonable question, Henri." she says. "Perhaps you should ask the gentleman, himself."
"I'm not finished…"
"Sorry, I thought you had," she says. "There's more?"
"Just this. Whatever happened to self-regulated avarice, self-imposed austerity, stoic restraint… that sort of thing?"

She smiles. "Stoic restraint is practiced religiously every day by the poor, but only out of necessity. Of the other two—self-regulated avarice never existed in this world. Self-imposed austerity is a dream undesirable to most and unattainable by others, which you alone envision because of your monk-like detachment from material things."
"Really?"
"In fact," she says sweetly.
"Your father, my father-in-law, says I have an unnatural resistance to joie of any sort. I've got joie don't I Sylvie?"

"Yes, Mon Ange, you've got joie. And because of you, I have it too. But," she explains nicely, "you should not deny my father his."

TUESDAY, very early morning

It's still dark out. Inside, in the bedroom, with the quiet ticking of the old clock, the chill, the open window, the dim light which reveals the cat snuggled up against Sylvie's legs, the dog curled up at the foot of the bed, Sylvie, like an angel, Henry on his back with his big mouth open, blankets up to their chins. We now find our way into Henry's mind where a cello plays. It comes up slowly underneath his snoring. It's simple music. But it's deep. Above all, it is beautiful. The volume increases, and in the dim light Henry looks angelic.
Well, pale anyway.

He's asleep but smiling. He opens his eyes, continues listening to the music. He recognizes the beauty of what he is hearing. He thinks he can play it. He explores that possibility for a moment. He starts to get up. He sits on the edge of the bed replaying the music in his head. The music fades as Sylvie stirs.
"Where are you going, Mon Ange?"
"Uh, I just need to…I need to try something out on the cello… before it…disappears on me."

He gets up and, straining to retain the music in his mind, he runs into the library and, stopping to listen to the music again, he grabs his cello. He sits; he cocks an ear. The music, though fragmented somewhat, rises again. He has the first note. He hums the first phrase. He puts a bow to his C string and… it breaks.

Henry's face is grotesque, it looks like the mask of TRAGEDY. He holds the limp end of the broken string in his hand. But he can no longer hold on to the music. It fades out quickly. Now, there's only silence. Dejectedly, Henry returns to bed. He looks at the clock, calculating how much longer until the violin shop across the bay opens.

TUESDAY AFTERNOON

Inside the fine violin shop instruments hang from the ceiling, like hams in a Spanish tavern. Henry walks in.

A tall young, unnecessarily handsome, noble-looking, long-haired creature—a GREAT violinist—is playing short, quick, extremely impressive passages on a violin. The shop manager—a man in an old plaid sports coat and mismatched bowtie—dotes upon the great violinist from behind the counter. A bent, frail, unassuming, old man— an instrument maker, in full-length leather apron—stands nearby in silent observation. The few other musicians in the shop—those who aren't purposefully pretending not to be impressed—all stand around at a respectful distance, agog and listening with open admiration. The women among them are swooning. The Great violinist stops playing, looks at the instrument with undisguised royal distaste.

"Is this the best you have for me?"
"At the moment… It is a truly exquisite instrument, Sir," says the shop manager with syrupy apology.
"What about the Guiseppi Fucelli?"
"Sold, last week… regrettably. I would have held it for you if you…"
"Sold?! You could have loaned it to **me**." The great violinist eyes some instruments mounted behind a glass case with cold disdain. He sighs.
"I'll be taking this one then, on loan for a while. If you get the Fucelli back—and, I'm sure you will make some effort (he raises one eyebrow) —perhaps you can ship it to me in Europe."
"It would be my pleasure of course, and… your Strad? What would you like us to ..?"
"Puhh." The great violinist postures. "Must you ask? I want only what any artist wants, what every artist has ever expected from an instrument: I wish a less tortured, more ethereal, high end. The instrument should surrender fully to me." He looks around at his admiring female followers. "The other must be…" He glances at his admirers, again, but with staged humility, "persuasive… but retaining dignity. Some cooperation from the instrument would be helpful in my quest to attain that."

He turns to the instrument maker. "We've made this request of you before, little man. We really wonder if you are listening. CAN you give me that?"
"Yes."
"WILL you give me that?"
"Yes… if it is possible."
"When can I expect to test this somewhat questionable assurance?"
The instrument maker looks to the shop manager, "I don't know… uh…"
The manager intervenes, "Soon." He smiles a broken smile.
It's clear that the great violinist doesn't like this response.
The manager corrects himself, "*Very* soon, Sir."

The instrument maker steps forward with his hand extended, "In the meanwhile, perhaps… the bow?"
The great violinist clutches his bow to his chest. "THIS bow, little man, is worth more than any instrument you have in this shop."
"Perhaps strings?" offers the shop manager quickly.
"You know very well that MY strings are made for me by Frederich Heiten… you should all have noted that… and were he here, he'd set-up my instrument the way **I** prefer it, not in whatever way best suits his convenience at the moment."

The great violinist eyes the bows that are set out before him on a velvet pad.
"I'll take these two on loan—have them sent—and I'll be back for my instrument Tuesday." He looks sternly at the instrument maker. "TUES-DAY, eh, little man?"
He turns crisply upon his heels to depart (carrying two violin cases under his arm). Every eye in the place is upon him.
Henry (of course) stands directly in his path.

The great violinist is glaring at Henry, who stands as if dazzled, frozen between the artist and the elevator. Then, Henry does what any reasonable man might naturally do, he smiles and says, "Hello."
The great violinist is far too aloof to respond in any way to such an idiotic gesture.

When the elevator chimes and the door begins to open, Henry realizes
the problem. (Ah!) He steps aside, holds the door for the great violinist,
leans in to push the down button for him, and smiles. But, the great
violinist is far beyond him, in thought, in stature, in every way.

The shop manager is worried. He turns to the instrument maker.
"What can we do for him?"
"I hesitate to do anything. That instrument has had that flat spot for
over 300 years. Others have tried everything that I might. I don't think
it'll brighten much under my hand."
They both stare at Henry for a while, without really seeing him.

After the instrument maker leaves, the shop manager continues to stare
at Henry without comment for a while. Eventually…the shop manager
resigns himself to dealing again with mere earth-bound beings. He does
so with grand indifference. "What can I do for you?"
Henry nods in the direction of the elevator. "Who was that guy?"
"*That guy* was Alexandre Linsky."
"Because, I have the same problem…"
"Same problem?"
"You know," says Henry nicely, "getting those highs to surrender, and
obtaining persuasive but dignified lows. I want that too. Well, I guess
it's what everybody really wants, has always wanted… but on my
cello."
The shop manager has nothing to say to this, no smile to offer. He
harbors no appreciation for wit, at the moment.

Henry slaps the broken string on the counter. "And I need a new C
string." He smiles. "But" he adds, "I really would like to get a little
more warmth out of my A as well."
The shop manager looks down upon Henry from a height only attained
by those who routinely grovel before the likes of Alexandre Linsky.
"Are you entirely sure it's the string?" he asks.

Henry—always appreciative of wit—nods and smiles nicely.
"OH, you think it might be my technique?" he asks, jovially.

The shop manager says nothing, turns around in place, goes to a drawer and withdraws a string. He opens another drawer and takes out another string. He turns and places them both on the counter.
"With skill you should be able to extract the warmth you seek from this. This C should do, as proper replacement for that one. If anything, it's superior. Is there anything else I may help you with?"

Henry hesitates, he ponders, he decides. "Well, uh… I've always wanted to try out one of your better cellos… you know, just to get it out of my system."
"You are welcome, of course, to do that."
"But, I don't have a bow. Maybe I'll pick up a bow, since I'm here."
"We have several nice bows, for cello, by Edmund Phipps."
"Can I have a look at one?"
"No."
"I can't even look at one?" Henry is confused.
"I'm sorry. They are reserved."
"Oh. OK. Well, do you have something I <u>can</u> look at?"
"Certainly."
Though it is painful for the man, he pulls open a drawer of bows and extracts one. "Many of our less-advanced cellists use this bow and find it suits their needs."

Henry picks up the bow and handles it.
"Can I try it out?"
The shop manager sighs heavily. "Certainly. We have a room for you back here."
"How much is this bow?"
"That one… is around 3200, I believe."
Henry places it back on the counter as though it were on fire.

Moments later, Henry is inside a small practice studio surrounded with cellos of every color. He is seated with cello and bow. He looks around beaming like a child in a toy store. After tuning it, he starts fiddling around, plucking the strings, cautiously spinning the instrument on its pin. First tentatively, then with mock aplomb, he begins to play. Soon he is playing seriously, first well, then increasingly better.

Finally, he finds himself playing the music that he heard in his head that morning. He's playing the piece with great passion and unbelievable skill. He's so deeply involved that he doesn't even notice how well he is playing. Engulfed in reverie, he plays the entire piece through. He then sits, suspended in ecstasy, thinking about the piece. He plays a few bars more before getting up, admiring the instrument, placing it in its stand gently, and emerging from the practice room.

Outside that room there is a small gathering: the shop manager, the instrument maker, two others. They are standing there stunned as he comes out. Others arrive from different parts of the shop.

The shop manager rushes to him eagerly and touches his elbow, as if to guide him through the throng.
"And, how did you find that instrument… Sir?"
Henry looks around somewhat surprised at the venerating crowd.
"It was a pleasure to play that thing."
"It was a pleasure to hear you play it, Sir," says the shop manager bowing. "And… the bow?"
Misunderstanding the man (that's just how humble he is) Henry quickly hands the man the bow. "I'm sorry. I was going to return it."
"No, no-no, Sir; I meant was the bow to your liking?"
"I prefer a little more tooth!" Henry declares with mock pretense.

The shop manager, bowing again, says, "Of course, many of the finest cellists do. Quite reasonable."

The small gathering watches dumbstruck as Henry is guided with great deference by the shop manager, down a hallway, toward the elevator.

Their faces display a single shared thought, "Wow, who was that guy?"

WEDNESDAY

They sit at the small table, strewn with dishes and cups. There are flowers. Henry is studying the French verb book, Sylvie is reading an old, nicely bound book.

Henry looks up and pauses. It's enough to get his dear wife's attention. "I've had a vision, Sylvie. For some time now, I've had this vision."

She places her elbows on the table, she rests her head in her hands and smiles a crumpled little smile. When he doesn't begin immediately, she raises her eyebrows, a signal to go ahead.
"OK, so forget that," he says, smiling apologetically.
She goes back to reading.

"Have you ever heard of a guy named Alexandre Linsky?" he asks.
Sylvie lowers her book.
"Oh yes, every woman in France is madly in love with that man."
"Really? Every woman in France?"
"Yes, every woman, every girl, every female. Perhaps some males as well. He is a great violinist and quite handsome and very rich and every woman in France is dying with passion for that man."
"I met him yesterday."
"You met Alexandre Linsky?"
"Yes, at the violin shop."
Sylvie puts down her book. "Why did you keep this from me, Henri?"
"Keep it from you…?"
"Why didn't you tell me that you met Alexandre Linsky?"
"I'm telling you now, Sylvie."
"But, truly? You met the violinist, Alexandre Linsky?"
"I did"
"Did you speak to him?"
"Yes. I said hello, but then I thought it would be a kindness to treat him just as if I didn't know who he was."
"Yes, that was kind of you. But, in reality you actually didn't know who he was, did you?"
"No, so, that made it pretty easy for me."
Henry reflects on the event for a bit.

"He plays a hell-of-a fiddle, that guy, I can tell you that. I wish you could have heard him."

"Oh-ho, and I wish that too," she says.

"And, I wish you could have heard me, Sylvie. I tried out one of their 10-times-what-my-cello-cost cellos, and when I finished playing everyone in the shop was standing around in awe."

"I'm sure they were, Mon Ange."

She goes back to her reading.

THURSDAY (Day of Miracles)

Henry is behind the wheel, downtown, and traffic is heavy. As he approaches an intersection the big black monster-like vehicle ahead of him slows to a stop. Henry waits, drumming with his thumbs upon the steering wheel; he's in no hurry; he's content; he has cello music in his head. The big black car in front of him is so big that Henry can see nothing beyond it. He can see the stop light hanging overhead if he leans over far enough. The light is green. He waits. The car in front of him starts through the intersection and Henry follows closely.

The car in front of him stops in the intersection, as the light turns yellow. Then, the light turns red, and the car turns, leaving Henry in the middle of the intersection with cars coming at him broadside, from both directions, horns blaring.

Henry speeds out of the intersection and is on his way when the inside of his car begins to pulse with a peculiar light, first reddish, then bluish, then reddish again. Behind him, as he can see in his rearview mirror, a motorcycle cop bumps his siren a couple of times. Henry sighs and pulls over into a bus stop.

Though not pleased, Henry continues drumming on the steering wheel, until the cop, wearing riding pants and tall shiny boots, arrives at his window.
"License and registration… please."
Henry recovers the registration from the glove compartment and his license, with some awkwardness from his front pocket, where he keeps his wallet. He hands them out the window to a gloved hand.

"Is it about that red light?" Henry asks.
"It is."
"Do I get a chance to explain?"
"You can explain to someone else at some other time."
"But, it's unfair."
"It always is."
"Can I explain anyway, and you just, you know, pretend to listen? I'd like to feel like I've been treated fairly."

"Go ahead. You have until I finish this…"
The cop begins writing in a thick tablet.

"I was behind this big, huge, monstrous truck-like thing and my nose
was already IN the intersection when the light turned yellow. THEN, he
moved forward a little bit and stopped—I don't know why—and I was
left there, hung up, IN the intersection when it turned red."
"Very nice," says the cop distracted. He hands the paperwork back to
Henry and continues writing in the tablet.
"Unfair is what it is," says Henry, "By rights HE should be getting the
ticket, not me. The guy in that huge stupid black truck-thing is the guy
that should be getting this ticket."

"Well, let's say I agree with you," says the cop as he tears something
from his tablet and hands it to Henry. Henry accepts it, looks at it,
tosses it on the seat beside himself. "Unless you can give me the license
plate number of that other vehicle, I can't really do anything about it,
can I?"
"Oh, I can give you the license plate number," says Henry. "It's 6EO
472."
"And how do you know that?"
"Well, I was looking at it as I was sitting there behind him. Once I see a
number, I remember it. I see it—BOOM—I remember it."
"So, you're one of those photographic memory guys, is that it?"
"No, it's a recently acquired skill. I just…"
"OK," says the cop, cutting him short, "so, now all I need is the type of
vehicle, make and model, and we're on our way."
"They all look alike to me," Henry shrugs. "But, PLEASE, can you
give me a break? It really *wasn't* my fault. I was *not* in any hurry, and I
wasn't *trying to* run a red light. It was just circumstance. Also, I don't
need this on my record."

"OK," says the cop, "Since you recall numbers so perfectly, I'll make a
deal with you. If you can tell me the number on the ticket, which you
just signed, I'll tear it up."
"Really?"
"I'm a man of my word."
"There were a lot of numbers on that thing."

"The one written along the side of the ticket in blue ink," says the cop smugly, while opening and glancing at his ticket book.

Henry closes his eyes, and casually, but with real enthusiasm, he recites, "4AB dash 0000 dash 6077 dash 1224 dash 1663 dash KA." In response, there is only silence from the cop, and no movement whatsoever.

The gloved hand comes into the car, palm up. The fingers wiggle. Henry recovers the ticket from the seat and places it in the glove. The cop tears it up. "Well," he says, "You're either what you say you are, or the luckiest man I ever met."
"Maybe both," says Henry. "Thank you."
"Drive carefully," says the cop and walks away. He salutes Henry as he slides by smoothly on his motorcycle.

To himself Henry says, "This is the luckiest day of my life." He puts the car in gear and, while looking back at traffic, pulls away from the curb slowly.

Out of the corner of his eye Henry detects movement. It's a kid on a bicycle. Henry slams on the brakes at the same time someone slaps the trunk of his car and shouts. "Hey!"

The kid is maybe 30 years old, riding a bicycle more suited to a 10-year-old, and giving Henry the finger with both hands, as he rides blindly into traffic. Henry shakes his head with a mix of admiration and disapproval as he watches the idiot/daredevil weave between cars.

Suddenly, Henry is thrown violently against the door of his car. There is a horn, the sound of crushing metal and shattering glass. Airbags go off and Henry is engulfed first in whiteness, then in blackness, then in whiteness again.

There's the sound of distant mumbled conversation.
There's a humming sound.
There's a steady beeping.

FRIDAY (delirium)

Between the beeps Sylvie says, "You really should try to get along with Papa, my love. Like it or not, we are all inextricably intertwined."
"Oh, I know it!" Henry tries to say, but no words come.

In M. Bouleau's opulent office Henry sits across from his father-in-law, who leans back with his hands interlaced behind his head. The desk between them is huge, ornate, cluttered with objects of various sorts. Bouleau says, "This is what I wanted to talk to you about. You are calling your wife SYL-vie, SYL-vie, comme ça… but her name is not SYL-vie. Her name is Sylvie. Sylvie, not SYL-vie; it's simple."
Henry stares at his father-in-law in disbelief.
"You're telling me how to pronounce my wife's name?"
Bouleau brushes off the question. He leans forward with both elbows on his desk. He is playing with something in his hands, reminiscing.

"As a child I always wanted a toy train" says Bouleau. "Oh, how I wanted that train. I wanted that train so badly. But, of course, we could never afford such a thing."
Henry says, just as a matter of fact, "We had a train set when I was a kid."
Bouleau stands up in a full rage.
"Well, good for you! Aren't you lucky?"

Now, there is more light in the room and more heat. More light, more heat. Henry discovers himself in the Bouleau's glass ceilinged ping pong room. M. Bouleau, across from him at the table, is aglow in sweat. Henry is bent practically in two, trying to catch his breath. Bouleau is laughing good naturedly. "So, how does it feel to be beaten by a man 20 years older than yourself?"
"You're not 20 years older than me," gasps Henry.

Bouleau throws his paddle onto the table in disgust. "Why do you choose to quibble on every matter no matter how small? How does it feel to be beaten by a man 17 years and several months older than yourself? Is that question more to your liking?" In passing, he rips the paddle from Henry's hand and tosses it on the table.

"This way you have of avoiding unsavory truth is too much like a child, Henri. You are too much like a child in that. Could you not have just shaken my hand, like a gentleman, like a true gentleman, and said, 'Congratulation, Monsieur, you have beaten me yet again.'? Could you not have laughed in a pleasant manner and said, 'Ah, Monsieur Bouleau, you have beaten me RESOUNDINGLY, yet again!'?"
Henry, still out of breath says, "I thought it was unnecessary."
"What did you say?"
Henry straightens up and looks Bouleau in the eye. "I said, I thought it was unnecessary to say."
"What do you mean by that?"
"I mean, it's not a great victory to beat a cellist at ping pong."
"Pah, you are not a cellist."

More light, more heat. More light, more heat, and Henry finds himself outside under a nice shade tree on a balmy afternoon, squinting into the sun. Now he is beside the great violinist. They sit together on a bench. The great violinist is being kindly, instructive…
"Of course. You don't use the full weight of the bow on every note, do you? So, it is foolishness to use the full width of the bow. Actually, they did a study of me when I was a child; filming my bowing technique, so many thousands of frames per second, and discovered an incredible range of angle and tilt and camber and… Of course, I was just starting out, but even then. There are times when my bow is laid entirely on edge, but a single horsehair upon the string. Immaculate." The great violinist reflects. "I really don't spend enough time just sitting around chatting with people of common stock."
"Do you think we could become friends?" asks Henry. "You could come over to our place for dinner when you're in town, or maybe, once in a while we could go out and shoot a little pool, grab a pizza an' a beer or something?"
"I'll have to speak with my manager about that; she can be quite stinting with my time. BUT, in the meantime how does *acquaintance* sound? You know, the sort of thing where your wife comes backstage after the concert and I greet her warmly..?"

There is more light, more heat. More light, more heat, and Henry finds himself seated in torment, next to his father-in-law.

They are chained together at the ankles, side by side, in HELL. They are dangling their feet—which glow like molten iron—in a slowly moving fiery stream. Behind his back voices whisper, "Nobody really likes him. Without sleep he turns snappish. He's mean spirited…"
Henry turns and declares, "I AM NOT."
Meanwhile, angels hover above Monsieur Bouleau, chanting, "He's so charming, so gracious. Yes, such a lovely man."

Without looking at the man Henry says, "Are we to spend the remainder of eternity, side by side, in blistering silence?"
Bouleau looks at him with venom in his eye, and says, "Why do you ask such things?"
"Because if it's gonna be just like home, I don't get the point."

They sit in silence, as the light and heat continue to build. Henry observes, "I know your *heart bled* when Sylvie told you of our plans to marry. And, apparently, it bled again when we did. But I never really understood why her happiness caused your poor old heart to bleed…"

More light, more heat, more light, more heat. More heat more heat more heat. Behind Bouleau the voices continue to sing, "So charming, so gracious, such a lovely man."

Walter appears, ambling by and stops long enough to lean over and whisper in Henry's ear: "Things would be different if dogs had access to lawyers. Oh my god, can you imagine?" He laughs and travels on. Walter shouts from the distance, "Dogs and lawyers, man!"

Henry observes, "So…your retirement and your death were the same event."
Bouleau responds, "I enjoyed my work."
"I know," says Henry. "I can understand that. But what was it that drove your desire to accumulate all that goddamned junk?"
"If you must ask, then you will never understand."
"I see." Henry reflects for a bit. "That's a reasonable French response."

They sit dangling their feet almost playfully in the molten river.

"What was it about our marriage that offended you so?"
"If you refuse to see it, I can not educate you on this matter."
 Henry gives that some thought.

"You haven't changed a bit," say Henry.
"Toi non plus," says Bouleau bitterly.
"The shame is…I think we could have been friends," says Henry.
"I agree with you entirely."
Henry is dumbfounded. "What did you say, Monsieur?"
"I agree with you entirely." Bouleau shrugs. "After all, I am not an unreasonable man."

The heat and the light disappear. Henry approaches a podium on stage, under a glaring spotlight. He shields his eyes, he clears his throat. "I've been working on this for a while," he says, and looks out into an ocean of empty theatre seats. "I've been preparing for this for a long time…" He closes his eyes, as if to gather his thoughts. He begins:

Je suis le Ténébreux, - le Veuf, - l'Inconsolé,
Le Prince d'Aquitaine á la Tour abolie
Ma seule Etoile est morte, - et mon luth constellé
Porte le Soleil noir de la Mélancolie.

Dans la nuit du Tombeau, Toi qui m'as consolé…

SATURDAY (At Home Again)

Opening his eyes, Henry sees the woman he loves sitting beside his bed. He's awash in the feelings that come from loving someone more than anything else in this world. It's clear from her eyes, her tears, her crumpled smile, that she shares that very same feeling.
"Where have you been my love?" she asks softly.
"I was in Hell," he says quietly. "And your father was there with me… of course."
Sylvie smiles and, bending close to him, kisses him gently on the cheek. "I was not in much better shape here, my very dear Henri."
"I'm in Heaven now," he says quietly.
"Yes. Welcome back," she says.

With her hand on his feverish brow she says, "While you were unconscious you were mumbling."
"Oh no. I've always feared this would happen. What was I mumbling?"
"Well, not mumbling really, you were enunciating quite precisely, actually, but so quietly, as if it were just for me."
"What was I mumbling quite precisely?"
"You were reciting a poem in French."
"Nonsense."
"Yes, you were, Henri. Gerard de Nerval. An extraordinary rendition too. I was in tears actually…for many reasons. But you did quite well. I was very proud of you. I was jealous of your teacher, of course."

"I've read that poem a thousand times, Sylvie, and I've thought about it since the day we were married. I'm scared to death at the thought of someday understanding it." He pauses, adrift in thought. "That was one of the 2400 reason I thought that maybe we shouldn't marry. That and living in the constant fear that people would see what a dolt I am."
"I live in constant fear that people may see how truly wonderful you are, Henri, and try to steal you away from me."

He holds up his hand and wrist, in a pure white cast.
"What happened to me?"

"You were in an accident… hit by a bus… and you have been
unconscious for a while, dear Henri. Considering the impact, the doctor
said it was miraculous that you only broke your wrist. That's the good
news."
"Hit by a bus," he says dreamily.
"The bad news: I'm afraid you won't be able to play the cello for a
while… or ping pong."
"I'll probably never speak French again either," he whispers.
"Oh-ho, I don't think a broken wrist should keep you from speaking
French, Henri," she scolds playfully.

M. Bouleau appears at the door with a bouquet of flowers, saying, "Oh,
you have decided to wake up after all."
"Well," says Henry, nonplussed by his father-in-law's appearance, "this
is a surprise…"
"Not at all," says Bouleau, "It is on my way home and I thought I
would stop in to see you. I have something I would like to say to you."
Henry anticipates a Hollywood ending. He smiles graciously. Sylvie is
expecting that as well. She is smiling, expectant.

"When you are feeling better," says Bouleau, "—only when you are
feeling up to it—please come by to help me in cleaning out my gutters.
It is not a two-man job, but it would be much easier for me if someone
were there, on the ground, to turn the hose on and off when I need it.
That way I will not have to go up and down the ladder so much, and
madame has other things to do."
Henry can think of nothing to say to this, and he says nothing.
Sylvie's reaction cannot be described. (That, I leave to you.)

"This is not something that needs immediate attention, of course,"
continues Bouleau, "but, when you have finished here, give me a call.
This accident of yours has been an inconvenience to us all."
Sylvie interrupts quickly to ask, "Those are very nice flowers, Papa,
where did you get them?"
Bouleau raises the flowers to take in their fragrance.
"Yes, I saw them in the little shop downtown. I thought they would
look quite nice on my desk at home. I didn't want to leave them in the
car to wilt."

He extends them toward Sylvie to appreciate. She smiles a crumpled little smile.

"So…" Bouleau says, wrapping up his visit, "No need to rush on the gutters; whenever you feel up to it." The man smiles. "It would be nice if you would call first, of course." He turns on his heels and, taking the flowers with him, departs.

Henry says nothing, stares into space without a word for a while.
"I adore you," Sylvie says, leaning in toward her husband. Henry smiles weakly.
"I'm very tired," he says. He closes his eyes from fatigue. He sleeps.

Sylvie places a hand on Henry's arm and pets him, as she tells him this story: "There was once a *very good* husband who went into town to trade the family cow.

Along the way he met a man who said, 'That's a pretty sad-looking cow; I'll trade you this fine goat for that cow.' And the good husband traded the sad cow for that fine goat.

Along the way he met another man who smirked and said, 'My dog is better than that old goat. Let me help you out; I'll trade this extraordinary dog for that miserable old goat.' And the good husband traded the old goat for the extraordinary dog and went on his way.

Then he was overtaken by a man, with a tortoise in a box. This man said, 'I am so glad I finally caught up with you. I saw you with that mangy looking dog—who obviously is not long for this world. How would you like to trade for this tortoise?—they are known to live forever.' And so, the good husband traded the dog—who was not long for this world—for the tortoise.

Arriving at last in town, the good husband went to the market and was about to trade the tortoise for something of great value, when he saw some lovely flowers that he knew his wife would enjoy. So, he traded the tortoise for those lovely flowers, and he started home.

Along the way, the good husband was run over by a run-away ox cart and the flowers were destroyed.

When he reached his village-home again, he came upon his friends leaning on a fence, talking. He told them about how he had traded the cow for a goat, and had traded the goat for a dog, and the dog for a tortoise, and the tortoise for the flowers that he knew his wife would enjoy. And he told them about how he had been run over by an ox cart and those lovely flowers had been destroyed.

These friends all laughed and jeered at him, saying, "Your wife is going to skin you alive!"

'Not at all,' declared the good husband boldly, 'my wife will be pleased just to have me home again.'

And he was right."

Sylvie leans close to her unconscious husband's ear, and she says this: "I don't care if you ever play the cello again; I don't care if you ever pick up another ping-pong paddle; I don't care if you never utter a single word in French for the remainder of our life together. I am pleased just to have you home again, Henri. I am very pleased."

SATURDAY EVENING

They are sitting together in their living room. He has a blanket thrown over him. The table next to him is cluttered with glasses and cups and notebooks.
"I don't know what got into me, Sylvie," says Henry. "I usually pay more attention when I'm driving."
Sylvie gets up to clear a few things from the table.
"About that, I have no doubt, Henri." She kisses him on the forehead.

While she carries things into the kitchen, Henry sits idly exploring his cast. He discovers that he cannot make any motion that might be useful in ping pong. Suddenly, his free hand goes unconsciously to his ear. He winces, cocks his head. He pushes the palm of his hand against his ear. He takes a napkin and rubs it against his ear and looks at it.

As she reenters the room Henry holds up the napkin. "Look at this... Sylvie, take a look at this."
She comes, she looks, she winces. "Euh, what is that?!"
"I have no idea. I found this little guy trying to crawl into my ear. What do you think it is?" He shows it to her again.
"Pouah! Henri, I think that's an earwig."
"Would you do me a favor, Sylvie, and throw it out the window?"

Sylvie, eyes averted, carries the napkin to the window, opens the window, and shakes it firmly several times. She's revulsed. She makes a face, she makes a noise, she crumples the napkin and, trembling, tosses it into a wastepaper basket. She turns toward her husband again and sits down, quivering with disgust.

On her back, clinging to her sweater, is (How did you guess?) …
the earwig.

"I'm glad I caught him," says Henry, "who knows what havoc he could have caused had he gotten into my ear."
"It certainly wouldn't have done you any good," she says, still shaking.

She quivers again, at the very thought.

115

SUNDAY MORNING

Sylvie is sitting with the cello in her hands, as if to play, when Henry emerges from the bedroom stretching and yawning. She's focused, tightening the bow. She stops when she sees him. She's a bit embarrassed.
"Sylvie?" he says teasingly. "When did you take up the cello?"
"I just thought I'd try it… since you won't be playing for a while. I'm so used to having the sound of it in our lives."
Henry is amused. He sits. He smiles. He gives her the go ahead in broad regal gestures.
"Well," Sylvie continues explaining, pursing her lips, "I've watched you do this so many times… and you always make it look so natural. I just thought…" She smiles apologetically.
"Maybe this would be a good time for me to teach you," he says. "Let's see what you can do."

She places the bow gently; she carefully places each finger of her fret hand. It's clearly the first time she's done any of this. Henry nods encouragingly and smiles with genuine admiration.

In the morning light, in that room, Sylvie looks like an angel—an angel with a cello. She cocks her head as if hearing something. She listens. She nods, she leans in.

Then she begins to play "SMILE"* so slowly, so deeply, so warm and beautifully. It's mesmerizing. Henry collapses into the big chair, closes his eyes, delighted, bewildered, awash in love for his very darling wife.

Unconsciously he rubs his ear.

THE END

[*Smile, by C. Chaplin]

A FINAL SHOT

Walter is sitting on a piece of cardboard in an alley. He's reading from
a tattered paperback book. He's greasy, he's dirty, he's got that slightly
crazed, challenging but clever, look in his eye.
He closes the book.
He leans toward us. He speaks.

Je suis le Ténébreux, - le Veuf, - l'Inconsolé,
Le Prince d'Aquitaine à la Tour abolie :
Ma seule Etoile est morte, - et mon luth constellé
Porte le Soleil noir de la Mélancolie.

Dans la nuit du Tombeau, Toi qui m'as consolé,
Rends-moi le Pausilippe et la mer d'Italie,
La fleur qui plaisait tant à mon coeur désolé,
Et la treille où le Pampre à la Rose s'allie.

Suis-je Amour ou Phébus ?... Lusignan ou Biron ?
Mon front est rouge encor du baiser de la Reine ;
J'ai rêvé dans la Grotte où nage la sirène...

Et j'ai deux fois vainqueur traversé l'Achéron :
Modulant tour à tour sur la lyre d'Orphée
Les soupirs de la Sainte et les cris de la Fée.

[El Desdichado, by Gerard de Nerval]

Mockridge also writes under the names; Henry Edward Fool, R I Mansfield,
Emma Moonsinger, and Charles, Dark-Cloud, Bellwether (depending upon his
mood, I suppose) Here is a list of some of his published work:

WHEN I WAS A LOW-LIFE: An American Education—by Henry Edward Fool
The culmination of nearly 50 years of writing—as well as occasional thought—
concerning 4 college years in Richmond, Virginia, beginning 1967.
WORDS FOR THIS CAN NOT BE FOUND: poetry of a sort by Henry Edward Fool
AN AMERICAN SAVAGE IN A FRENCH HOTEL: An Accurate Accounting of the
Various Reasons I Should Be Hung -by Henry Edward Fool
Concerning 12 years working in a small privately owned French Hotel, in San Francisco.
EARWIG: originally included "Jack Nicholson IS Santa Claus"- by Darryl Mockridge
AMERICAN RACONTEUR: Real American Writin' for Real American Readin' by
Henry Edward Fool
Concerning events 18 years prior to, and the nearly 40 years after the events recorded in
When I Was A Low-Life
LOST IN THE DIN: Why Your Opinion on Politics and Religion Means NOTHING, and
mine means even less - by Henry Edward Fool
Politics as seen from a particularly honest POV
REFINEMENT: How a Good Marriage Can Nudge an Unwary Man in the Direction of
Civility - by Henry Edward Fool
Concerning (yes, I'm as surprised as you are) marriage.
QUIT SMOKING in 17 DAYS, if you truly wish to- by Darryl Mockridge
(a booklet for smokers who are too intelligent to continue nursing that mindless habit.)
TWO WEEKS IN BLETANTE - by Darryl Mockridge
A visit to a non-existent island nation reveals the fact that law and common sense need
not necessarily be, in every instance, mutually exclusive.
RETURN TO BLETANTE - by Darryl Mockridge
Previously expelled from Bletante–and set adrift at sea in a rubber raft—Mockridge finds
himself invited back, this time as a Greatly Honored Guest of the Island Nation.
WHY GOD GAVE US GUNS, and other stories without meaning - by Darryl Mockridge
Mockridge explains Political/Social situations in the US, at a time when the madness had
just begun—you know, before the big sneeze—through easily digestible stories.
AMERICA, as I know it- by R I Mansfield
Merely, solely, and nothing more than a collection of stories about my personal
experiences regarding a variety of things that seem to be nagging some of us these days
(race, drugs, guns, that sort of thing).

[You don't have to buy these things—you can read any of them, in their entirety, on
estuarypublications.com, by simply clicking on the cover.]

9 781723 863240